BFI Film Classics

CW00541086

The BFI Film Classics is a series of books that introduces, interprets and celebrates landmarks of world cinema. Each volume offers an argument for the film's 'classic' status, together with discussion of its production and reception history, its place within a genre or national cinema, an account of its technical and aesthetic importance, and in many cases, the author's personal response to the film.

For a full list of titles available in the series, please visit our website: <www.palgrave.com/bfi>

'Magnificently concentrated examples of flowing freeform critical poetry.'
Uncut

'A formidable body of work collectively generating some fascinating insights into the evolution of cinema.'
Times Higher Education Supplement

'The series is a landmark in film criticism.'
Quarterly Review of Film and Video

Star Wars

Will Brooker

A BFI book published by Palgrave Macmillan

First published in 2009 by
PALGRAVE MACMILLAN

on behalf of the

BRITISH FILM INSTITUTE
21 Stephen Street, London W1T 1LN
www.bfi.org.uk

There's more to discover about film and television through the BFI. Our world-renowned archive, cinemas, festivals, films, publications and learning resources are here to inspire you.

Palgrave Macmillan in the UK is an imprint of Macmillan Publishers Limited, registered in England, company number 785998, of Houndmills, Basingstoke, Hampshire RG21 6XS. Palgrave Macmillan in the US is a division of St Martin's Press LLC, 175 Fifth Avenue, New York, NY 10010. Palgrave Macmillan is the global academic imprint of the above companies and has companies and representatives throughout the world. Palgrave® and Macmillan® are registered trademarks in the United States, the United Kingdom, Europe and other countries.

Series cover design: Ashley Western
Series text design: ketchup/SE14
Images from *Star Wars*, Lucasfilm Ltd/Twentieth Century-Fox Film Corporation; *The Searchers*, C.V. Whitney Pictures Company/Warner Bros.; *Lawrence of Arabia*, © Horizon Pictures (G.B.); *633 Squadron*, © Mirisch Corporation of Delaware; *THX 1138: 4EB*, American Zoetrope; *American Graffiti*, Universal Pictures/Lucasfilm Ltd/Coppola Company; *Star Wars Episode II Attack of the Clones*, © Lucasfilm Ltd.

Set by Cambrian Typesetters, Camberley, Surrey
Printed in China

This book is printed on paper suitable for recycling and made from fully managed and sustained forest sources. Logging, pulping and manufacturing processes are expected to conform to the environmental regulations of the country of origin.

British Library Cataloguing-in-Publication Data
A catalogue record for this book is available from the British Library

ISBN 978–1–84457–277–9

Contents

Acknowledgments

I have a substantial collection of BFI Film Classics on my bookshelf, their spines arranged in a spectrum of colour, and it is a great privilege to be able to add my own monograph to this prestigious list, alongside the work of authors and scholars I have respected for decades.

My thanks go to those at the BFI and Palgrave who gave me this opportunity: Sarah Watt, who first discussed the proposal, Rebecca Barden, who saw it through, and the anonymous readers who responded both critically – making this a better book than it would have been – and positively, encouraging me towards its completion.

I am grateful to my friends and colleagues in Film and Television at Kingston University: particularly Frank Whately, who supported my research leave in summer 2008, Abbe Fletcher, for sharing her expertise on Brakhage, and Simon Brown, who led the field in my absence.

Above all, as ever and always, thanks to my family.

Introduction

Star Wars created soldiers. It created psychologists, Christians and artists. It created film-makers. It must also have created film academics. It was certainly the first film I took detailed notes on, in the dark, during a 1980 rescreening at London's Institute of Contemporary Arts. I scribbled down dialogue and sketched details like helmet insignia and computer displays; a junior anthropologist snatching field-notes from this rich alien world. The sequel, *The Empire Strikes Back* (1980), was the first film I considered in terms of its production – realising the negotiation, experiment and physical labour that lay behind the finished image – and after reading Alan Arnold's making-of account, *Once Upon a Galaxy* (1980),[1] I put those ideas into action on a small scale, filming my own version of the Bespin carbon-freezing chamber using stop-motion Super-8, figurines and indoor fireworks. Finally, *Return of the Jedi* (1983) was the first film that engaged me in investigative speculation around secondary texts and paratexts, as, aged thirteen and treating the project with at least as much diligence as any homework, I tried to piece together the final episode from pre-production sketches and interviews with crew members.

So, with hindsight, *Star Wars* made me a film scholar. I can't be the only one. And yet film scholarship has largely dismissed *Star Wars* in the thirty-plus years since its release. This book is meant as a first step toward redressing that.

It may seem a surprising claim and an unnecessary effort. Surely there are more than enough books on *Star Wars*? Yes, there are a lot of books on *Star Wars*. There is a small library of books on *Star Wars*, in my house alone. There are histories of the film's production and reception; encyclopaedias of every alien, droid and planet in the sequels, the prequels, the canonical mythos and its spin-offs; complete scripts illustrated with pre-production paintings; hardcover guides to ship designs, weapons specs and location cutaways; catalogues of posters, toys and collectables. These books reveal the true names of the cantina creatures, the evolution of Darth Vader's costume and the future of Leia and Han's children, but needless to say, they are intended for the fan's bedroom, not the lecture theatre or university library.

Cinema scholarship seems embarrassed by *Star Wars* – embarrassed that a movie series so popular, successful and influential is also, apparently, so childishly simple – to the extent that it primarily discusses the film in relation to its audiences, special effects, merchandising, ownership or influence on the studio system, rather than in terms of narrative, performance, cinematography, direction or editing. That is, academia rarely engages with *Star Wars* as a film text, as opposed to a cultural phenomenon; any discussions of its themes, story and character tend to be either patronising or contemptuous.

For instance, major guides and reference works such as Pam Cook and Mieke Bernink's *The Cinema Book*,[2] David Bordwell and Kristin Thompson's *Film History*,[3] Bordwell and Thompson's *Film Art*,[4] John Hill and Pamela Church Gibson's *Oxford Guide to Film Studies*[5] and Joanne Hollows, Peter Hutchings and Mark Jancovich's *Film Studies Reader*[6] only mention *Star Wars* in terms of studios, institutions and technology, rather than film form. Thomas Schatz's 1993 essay 'The New Hollywood' in Jim Collins, Hilary Radner and Ava Preacher Collins's *Film Theory Goes to the Movies* provides a particularly vivid example of this approach: while it gives details of *Star Wars*' 1977 and 1978 box office, its reissues, its longevity as a franchise and its influence on cinema sound systems, Schatz dismisses the film's story and themes as 'remarkably superficial … character depth and development are scarcely on the narrative agenda'.[7]

Similarly, Geoff King's book *New Hollywood Cinema: An Introduction* (2002) spares only a brief glance at *Star Wars* outside the context of special effects, sound and box-office takings:

comparing the film to *The Searchers* (1956) and *Taxi Driver* (1976), King concludes that, unlike the more complex films it in some ways resembles, it has no 'moral ambiguity' and concerns itself only with 'straightforward, innocent and fresh-faced heroics'.[8] This is a common view of *Star Wars*, and one that my approach will challenge.

Finally, Robin Wood's substantial chapter on *Star Wars* in *Hollywood from Vietnam to Reagan … and Beyond* first appeared in 1986, but its arguments against the original trilogy tally closely with those discussed above: that is to say, there has been little advance on them in the last twenty years. For Wood, *Star Wars* is efficient on a simple level, reconstructing the viewer as a child and providing reactionary, 'mindless and automatic pleasure'.[9] The films are 'intellectually undemanding', and invite the viewer to let 'Uncle George take you by the hand and lead you through Wonderland'.[10] Wood, who carelessly spells key characters' names incorrectly even in his revised edition, finds it impossible to imagine that anyone returns to *Star Wars* to discover 'new meanings, new complexities, ambiguities, possibilities of interpretation'[11] – although ironically, he offers one of the most insightful readings in existing scholarship of the film's ambivalent attitude towards fascist iconography and, in turn, its theme that totalitarianism can arise within the forces of 'good'. My approach will demonstrate that (as Wood in fact suggests himself) further examination of the film does reveal complex ambiguities and internal contradictions.

So there are many popular, fan-oriented books about the close detail of *Star Wars*, as a saga of six films and an Expanded Universe of spin-offs; and there are academic books that discuss *Star Wars* as a cultural event, largely in terms of its effects – literally, its special effects, but also its consequences for the studio system, for the blockbuster, for cinema sound, for fandom and merchandising. What I am doing here is different, and can be summed up in four words and a date:

Star Wars: George Lucas (1977).

This book is a study of *Star Wars* at the point when that was its only title – when it had not been repositioned as 'Episode IV: A New Hope'. While it also offers an interpretation of the film's motifs and themes within the broader arc of the six-episode saga, it focuses primarily on *Star Wars* as a film George Lucas directed in 1977, in the context of the films he had made up to that point, and the films that influenced both *Star Wars* and his earlier work – not as a game of spot-the-postmodern-pastiche, but as a reconstruction of the cinema that, in some cases subconsciously, shaped Lucas's approach to direction, performance, lighting, shooting and editing.

As suggested above, my approach will also suggest that *Star Wars* is not the straightforward, simplistic morality tale and fairy story that it is often described as – and derided as – in academic study. One of the key aspects of my argument is that *Star Wars* is not, as Lucas himself has claimed, a radical departure from his earlier work, but that it continues the experiments with sound and image that he began as a student at the University of Southern California (USC) and continued through his first two features, *THX 1138* (1971) and *American Graffiti* (1973), and shows the influence of Eisenstein, Norman McLaren, cinéma vérité and *Alphaville* (1965) as well as Kurosawa, David Lean, the Western and *The Dam Busters* (1955). It is a film conflicted by Lucas's need for total ownership and disciplined control of his work – the mode he became accustomed to as a one-man creator of short, avant-garde animations – and his contradictory desire for human warmth, community and improvisation.

Star Wars reveals the clash between Lucas's pleasure in the exterior, reflective surfaces of objects, and his enjoyment in taking them apart and customising them; his admiration for raw documentary, and his obsession with polished, high production values; his nostalgia for classical Hollywood adventure and his interest in abstract formalism; his aspiration to create a Hawksian or Godardian gang, and his preference for cutting film alone, rather than dealing with other people. In summary, *Star Wars* is made fundamentally problematic – and fascinating – by the fact that Lucas is invested in, and sympathetic to, the coldly organised aesthetic of the Empire, as well as the raw improvisation of the Rebels.

I draw out these conflicts and contradictions by looking at *Star Wars* in a way that, astonishingly, has not been attempted before; by studying it closely as a film, in terms of its cuts, compositions, costumes, soundtrack and *mise en scène*. Ironically, my engagement with *Star Wars* draws on ideas of auteurism and structural opposition – precisely the approaches that film scholarship employed in the late 1960s and early 1970s, when *Star Wars* was just a note on Lucas's yellow writing pad, to elevate the Western from its status as commercial entertainment to something worthy of serious study (see Jim Kitses's *Horizons West* from 1969,[12] and Will Wright's *Sixguns & Society: A Structural Study of the Western* from 1975).[13] Perhaps, then, this book comes thirty years late. But it is a start.

1 Before *Star Wars*

Before *Star Wars* was *The Emperor*.

In the revised chronology of Lucas's completed saga of course, *Star Wars Episode IV* is preceded by *The Phantom Menace* (1999), *Attack of the Clones* (2002) and *Revenge of the Sith* (2005), but in real terms Lucas had made nine short films and three features before 1977, including *The Emperor* (1967), a celebration of local DJ Bob Hudson.

Lucas's student films at the University of Southern California, where he was enrolled as an undergraduate from 1964–6, and then as a postgraduate during 1967, included vérité and formalist experiment, animation and conventional action-movie editing, sometimes in the same short project. *Look at Life* (1965) is a rapid-paced, stop-motion montage of magazine images, cut to a frantic beat. *Herbie* (1966) offers, in the words of the title card, 'moments of reflection'[14] that focus on the polished surface of a car at night, shot in cool black and white with a jazz soundtrack. *Freiheit* (1965) is a vignette about a young man racing for an unidentified border, mown down by a uniformed guard at the last second, while *1:42.08* (1966) tracks a bright yellow racing car around its circuit. The short *6.18.67* (1967) is Lucas's "desert poem",[15] a distant observation of another film, J. Lee Thompson's *Mackenna's Gold* (1969) during production, and *filmmaker* (1968) records Lucas's experience of working on Coppola's *The Rain People* (1969). His 1967 *anyone lives in a pretty (how) town*, loosely adapting verse by e.e. cummings, animates human beings in a coldly whimsical fable. Finally, the most significant work of Lucas's early career is *THX 1138: 4EB* (1967), which combines picture and sound distortion with a science-fiction escape thriller.

These films, despite their variation and diversity, are grouped together in the official history of Lucas's career – one constructed to an extent by the director himself, but also supported by his friends and colleagues – as his 'experimental' period. This history, as repeated across biographies, interviews and behind-the-scenes documentaries, is that Lucas was an experimental film-maker who went radically off-track with the mainstream space opera of *Star Wars* and has never achieved his frequently stated aim to get back to this earlier, more challenging and alternative mode. It is often implied that this failure represents a loss to cinema of a genuinely original, innovative film-maker, rather than a purveyor of family fantasy, computer-generated imagery (CGI) concoctions and corporate merchandising.

For example, Lucas's friend and collaborator John Milius spoke in 1998 of the 'great loss' that 'George stopped making movies, and got interested in the sort of stuff that Lucasfilm puts out. Because he was a really dynamic filmmaker.'[16] Similarly, Francis Ford Coppola, Lucas's one-time mentor, told the BBC's *Omnibus* team in 1997 that

George was one of the most talented American film directors of that time, and somehow, with the great success of *Star Wars*, we were deprived of those films he was going to make, and might have made, and instead we have an enormous industrial marketing complex.

The cut to obese crime lord Jabba the Hutt at this point seems deliberate. Coppola goes on:

I do hope that George Lucas the *filmmaker* finally emerges ... and goes his own way, against perhaps the wishes of George the entrepreneur. No matter how many billions of dollars *Star Wars* could earn, and no matter how valuable that franchise that they call is [sic] it isn't worth a tenth of what he's worth as an artist, and what he's capable of doing.

Rick McCallum, producer of the *Star Wars* saga, echoes Coppola: 'I think once we've finished these prequels, [Lucas] will start to do the more interesting experimental films he's always wanted to do.'

Perhaps surprisingly, Lucas agrees that *Star Wars* represents a diversion from his previous, 'experimental' cinema – although, like the *Star Wars* films themselves, his retelling of his personal history has undergone revisions during the last three decades. Even in 1974, when his space fantasy was still in production as *The Star Wars*, *Film Quarterly* reported that Lucas 'hopes to do more experimental work in the future', yet 'does not feel he is compromising in making more straightforward entertainment movies'.[17] By 1980, with the release of *The Empire Strikes Back*, Lucas had decided it was time to return to the USC mode of film-making. As he told *Rolling Stone*:

I loved shooting *cinéma vérité* and thought I would become a documentary filmmaker. [...] I don't want to be a businessman. My ambition is to make movies, but all by myself, to shoot them, cut them, make stuff I want to, just for my own exploration, to see if I can combine images in a certain way. My movies will go back to the way my first films were ...[18]

A year later, struggling with the script for what was then *Revenge of the Jedi*, he confirmed in an interview with *Starlog* that when he enrolled at USC:

I wanted to be a cameraman ... my first films were very abstract – tone poems, visual. [...] I decided to go back to graduate school ... and did many more movies, but still non-story type films. I was interested in abstract, purely visual films and cinéma-vérité documentaries.[19]

However, while acknowledging that his life had taken a surprising path, the George Lucas of 1981 seemed sanguine about having ended up in mainstream, blockbuster film-making.

My goals were to make bizarre abstract movies, and I expected to end up a documentary film-maker and work for a television station or something. I don't know if I'd have been completely happy at it ... I just sort of overshot my target – in a rather major way. [...] As corny as it sounds, the power of positive thinking goes a long way.[20]

At this point, despite the trials of the ongoing production, *Star Wars* is presented confidently as an achievement beyond Lucas's expectations; it was not his original goal, but it arrived as a combination of happy accident and 'positive thinking'.

By 1983, according to Michael Kaminski, 'the small-town experimental filmmaker had grown into the biggest movie mogul on the planet and the Lucasfilm kingdom occupied his every waking hour'.[21] In May of that year, Lucas bitterly admitted to *Time* that

the sacrifice I made for *Star Wars* may have been greater than I wanted ... it's an interesting choice I made, and now I'm burned out. In fact, I was burned out a couple of years ago, and I've been going on momentum ever since. *Star Wars* has grabbed my life and taken it over against my will. Now I've got to get my life back – before it's too late!

But of course, Lucas failed, once again, to abandon *Star Wars* and return to his previous, small-scale and alternative mode; instead, he returned to the original trilogy and revamped it with new scenes and CGI effects. In 1998, when the Special Editions were released in cinemas, Lucas was contemplative, expressing doubts about his career trajectory but seeing it as the result, for good or bad, of his own artistic choices. 'Ultimately, my life has taken a very funny twist from where I expected to go ...' he told *Omnibus*, 'and I'm not sure why, other than I did what I wanted to do, and I was making the movie I wanted to make.'

Seven years later, Lucas had finished directing the second trilogy of 'prequels', and the saga was finally complete. A 2005 *Wired* feature by Steve Silberman, based on an extensive interview, presents the director once again 'at a crossroads', regretting his detour from experimental work and preparing to return to his roots. 'I like *Star*

Wars,' Lucas muses, 'but I certainly never expected it would take over my life.' Silberman consults former colleagues and mentors, who – like Coppola and McCallum in the 90s – express concern about Lucas's recent path. Walter Murch, Lucas's sound designer from the early 1970s, wagers that 'if George were here and we could wrestle him onto the carpet, he'd say, "Yeah, I've gotten into that box, and now I want to get out of that box."' Lucas's former cinematography instructor, Woody Omens, is

proud of George, but I'm worried about him. He was trying to speak a different cinematic language at an early point in his career, and he's still trying to get to that. If he wanted me to mentor him again 40 years later, I would say, 'Let go. Do something that explores the non-narrative side of human expression from the perspective of a master and a veteran ...'.[22]

'For the past couple of years,' Silberman reports, Lucas has 'been telling interviewers that the breakout popularity of *American Graffiti* in 1973 "derailed" him into the business of mass-market filmmaking and that his career was "sidetracked" by *Star Wars*'.

Lucas and his contemporaries came of age in the 1960s vowing to explode the complacency of the old Hollywood by abandoning traditional formulas for a new kind of filmmaking based on handheld cinematography and radically expressive use of graphics, animation, and sound. But Lucas veered into commercial moviemaking, turning himself into the most financially successful director in history by marketing the ultimate popcorn fodder.

Now he has returned to the most private place in his universe to reinvent himself. He could spend the rest of his life capitalizing on *Star Wars'* legacy. Instead he's trying to dream up a second chance to be the rebel filmmaker he aspired to become a long time ago.[23]

In Silberman's account, Lucas's rebellion was first crushed by the Old Hollywood studios – 'the Empire struck back' when Warners insisted on making cuts to *THX 1138*, and Universal threatened not to release *American Graffiti* – and then subsumed by his 'inner Vader', a reading suggested by Lucas's admission during a 2004 documentary that as the head of a corporation, 'I have become the very thing that I was trying to avoid. That is Darth Vader … .'

This history of Lucas's career relies on three interlinked premises: first, that Lucas's student films were exclusively experimental in their use of cinéma vérité and abstract form; second, that *Star Wars* consists of 'popcorn fodder', offers nothing but unadventurous, mainstream storytelling and represents a significant departure from Lucas's student films; and third, that the radical shift from the first type of cinema to the second began with *American Graffiti*.

In the main body of this study, I will demonstrate more fully the continuities between Lucas's student films and *Star Wars*. His USC work is, without a doubt, more obviously experimental than the features, but I will show that Lucas's entire early oeuvre, from 1966 to 1977 – the USC films, the first two features and *Star Wars* itself – combines conventional, classical Hollywood technique with approaches inspired by French, Japanese and Soviet cinema, vérité documentary, and the formalist avant-garde.

As suggested above, the 'experimental' work that Lucas, according to his own testimony as well as those of his friends, supposedly abandoned during the mid-1970s, already exhibits elements of mainstream technique. *Freiheit*, though it concludes with distorted voiceovers discussing the meaning of freedom and depicts the climactic shooting through a quick-fire montage of still images, is skilfully cut for suspense and employs conventional Hollywood form to draw the viewer immediately into the story: the boy's sprint through the forest is constructed of quick, varied shots (a crash zoom, a whip-pan, a snatched close-up of feet splashing through a puddle, a long shot to establish the scene) joined through matches on action, and we are invited to identify with the protagonist through point-of-view shots of the border coupled with close-ups of his wild-eyed, anxious face. Similarly, though *1:42.08* is cited by John Baxter as an example of Lucas's cold preference for machines over humans – 'the film has no character except the car'[24] – its rapid editing also draws us into an identification with the driver through point-of-view shots and close-ups of his face that are clearly, causally linked to long shots of the vehicle: a glimpse of the driver's hands wrenching the wheel to the right cuts to a shot of the car rounding a sharp bend, and the driver's grimace precedes a frustrating spin-out. The short film shows an expert understanding of Hollywood action film editing, reminiscent of the World War II movies Lucas studied and re-edited in preparation for the *Star Wars* dogfights.

Similarly, it is too easy to see the feature film *THX 1138* as the last gasp of Lucas's experimental spirit, and *American Graffiti* as his shift into optimistic, light-hearted and commercial movie-making. This, again, has become accepted as the official history. Garry Jenkins's biography of Lucas describes *THX* as 'a bleak, Orwellian mood piece. Science fiction it may have been, *Star Wars* it was not.'[25] By contrast, Alan Ladd, head of production at Twentieth Century-Fox, compared the Anchorhead scenes from *Star Wars* to '*American Graffiti* in outer space', suggesting a bridge between the second and third features.[26] Lucas himself, looking back, links *THX* to his USC work rather than to *Star Wars*:

My vision was not to do a normal story. I wanted to do something that was abstract, much more like a student film than a [conventional] drama. Obviously, to get it through the studios, it had to be a drama, but by this time *Easy Rider* had come out, so we thought, 'Maybe we can get away with a really wacky, avant-garde film.'[27]

Dale Pollock's biography, *Skywalking*, presents Lucas's decision to make *American Graffiti* as a deliberate attempt to change the way he was perceived as a director – 'Lucas wanted to make a movie that would dispel his image as a technobrat, a cold, mechanical filmmaker devoid of warmth and humor'[28] – and Lucas suggests that the film was made in response to a challenge from Coppola.

I was getting a lot of razz from Francis and a bunch of friends who said that everyone thought I was cold and weird and why didn't I do something warm and human ... I thought, 'you want warm and human, I'll give you warm and human'.[29]

THX, according to Lucas, gave him a reputation as 'a cold, weird director, a science-fiction sort of guy who carried a calculator.'

So I thought, maybe I'll do something exactly the opposite. If they want warm human comedy, I'll give them one, just to show that I can do it. *THX* is very much the way I am as a film-maker. *American Graffiti* is very much the way I am as a person – two different worlds.[30]

This interpretation suggests that – rather than Lucas breaking cleanly away from his previous work with *American Graffiti* and abandoning the approach of *THX* for a 'warm and human' tone that then goes on to influence *Star Wars* – the director's first two features directly inform the opposing sides of *Star Wars*, shaping two very different worlds in conflict. The youthful optimism of *American Graffiti* would, in this analysis, feed directly into the raw energy of the Rebellion, and the colder, more clinical environments of *THX* would become the Imperial Death Star.

This is a more accurate reading, but we should not be led to exaggerate the difference between Lucas's first two features, and in doing so, simplify them both. While the full-length *THX* does inherit the formalist foregrounding of abstract imagery – CCTV interference, computer digits filling the screen – from *THX 1138: 4EB*, it also expands on the short film's underlying chase-and-escape structure, with its climactic bike pursuit (shot and cut, like *1:42.08*, with the panache of conventional Hollywood) serving as a clear precursor not just to *Return of the Jedi*'s speeder bikes and *The Phantom Menace*'s pod race, but also the light cycles of *Tron* (1982) and the chase scenes in mainstream, commercial SF like *Judge Dredd* (1995), *Minority Report* (2002) and *I, Robot* (2004). Moreover, it shares with *American Graffiti* (and Lucas's previous films like *6.18.67*) a documentary approach, its distant cameras allowing the actors to improvise naturalistic dialogue: though the social structure depicted in *THX* is restrictive and repressive, the film is about the failure of that society to fully control rebellious energy, and Donald Pleasance's performance in the White Limbo prison zone includes hesitations, slurs and swallowed words.

American Graffiti, in turn – while it aims throughout for easy, careless naturalism – also drops the viewer into a community whose customs and vocabulary are initially alien, and like *THX* the film involves extensive, experimental play with sound montage and distortion: each rock'n'roll track was 'worldised', re-recorded by Lucas and Walter Murch so it warped and echoed across streets and dance-halls.

As Lucas predicted himself prior to its release, *Star Wars* would mesh elements of his two previous features. 'Take the first two and combine them with another side of me that hasn't been seen yet and you get this new film.'[31] *Star Wars* represents the synthesis of Lucas's film-making at that point in his career: the surveillance culture of the Death Star is inherited from *THX* and the teen banter from *American Graffiti*, but the sound montage, the *in medias res* immersion in a strange culture, the fascination with machines – both their shiny surfaces and their inner workings – the underlying theme of escape, and the documentary approach, with its implications for naturalistic, improvisational performance, are common to both – and all these elements can be traced back in turn to aspects of the student films.

Yet *Star Wars* is not quite like the two previous features; it adds something new, and like *American Graffiti*, it was – according to Lucas – a deliberate challenge to push himself into unfamiliar territory. 'I thought before I retire,' he told *Starlog*, 'I want to make one real movie – you know, on sound stages with sets, the way they used to make movies.'[32] While not the radical departure from his earlier cinema that some histories imply, *Star Wars* did – as Lucas suggests here – draw more extensively on classical Hollywood than his previous work; that is, it paid greater homage to the films he enjoyed on TV when he was a child, rather than the experimental, avant-garde, documentary and international cinema he had first encountered at USC.

The real difference, though, lay not just in the budget and the shift away from guerrilla shooting 'in the streets, using absolutely nothing'[33] to the more ambitious and lavish methods of classical cinema. As he explained to *Écran*:

I come from experimental cinema, it's my specialty ... THX 1138 was a non-narrative film, a film without a framework. *American Graffiti* was similar; it was a juxtaposition of different sequences rather than one coherent story. On the other hand, *Star Wars* is a classic story, an old-style narrative ... I wanted to know if I could do it. I wanted to explore this creative field that I had consciously avoided. It's really what I wanted to do: be the sole architect of a traditional story where everything was linked by cause and effect.[34]

The one element that *Star Wars* genuinely introduces to Lucas's work, and that his previous films, from shorts to features, all lack, is a direct, linear and conventional storyline, created through the condensation of several earlier adventure stories into a powerful narrative structure: the simple fable of a young man leaving his home, finding his destiny, assembling a team and taking up the fight against an enemy. Its explicit aim was to provide a modern fairy story for a generation that had grown up without them. 'And kids need fairy tales – it's an important thing for society to have for kids.'[35] As Pollock summarises:

Lucas wanted to return to more traditional values that held a special appeal for our rootless society. He needed a timeless fable that could demonstrate, not pontificate on, the differences between right and wrong, good and evil, responsibility and shiftlessness.[36]

'There was no modern mythology to give kids a sense of values, to give them a strong mythological fantasy life,' Lucas confirmed.

'Westerns were the last of that genre for Americans.'[37] *Star Wars* was made to fill that gap. As a fable, a story of simple and readily understood oppositions, it creates a clear distinction between the good guys and the bad, and the aesthetic of the Rebels is, for the most part, visibly different from that of the Empire. The film's central theme of escape, rebellion and destiny is common also to *THX 1138* and *American Graffiti*, but the earlier features, with no claims to be modern-day fables, offer subtler shades of grey in place of *Star Wars'* black and white; THX himself is a part of the society that seeks to control him, whereas *American Graffiti'*s Curt has to struggle against his doubts and fears, rather than cops and street gangs.

To make *Star Wars'* battle lines immediately clear, Lucas ranges elements from his previous films on each side of the galactic conflict as if lining up pieces on a chess set. The Rebels are associated with documentary improvisation, customisation and the make-do camaraderie of the Hollywood war film and Western; the Empire draws on a colder, more disciplined use of human figures in formal patterns, enjoying technology for its reflective surfaces rather than for the creative potential of its inner workings, and returning to the bleak structures of both *THX* films, which in turn draw on the European SF of *Alphaville*.

What should now be obvious – and what makes *Star Wars* a more complex piece of work than even the director seems to realise – is that in this supposedly clear-cut conflict between good and evil, *Lucas is rooting for both sides.*

2 Dirt

Dirt, trash, scuffs, scratches. The desert-battered surface of Luke's
landspeeder, and the worn, washed-out fabric of his farmer's clothes,
bound and belted against the sand. Han Solo's outfit, a collage of
trophies and souvenirs from a past on both sides of the law, from
the Imperial Academy to the Corellian spacers, and his customised
'piece of junk' pirate ship. This is the aesthetic of the Rebels.
A make-do-and-mend approach, in a time of galactic war.
An attitude of improvisation, of rolling with the punches, of
striking, scattering and moving on. The Rebels are freedom fighters,
or terrorists, depending on your point of view: they are potentially
everywhere, and hard to pin down. Leia can give up the location of a
previous base on Dantooine, knowing the Empire will find only
deserted buildings and footprints. They establish a new headquarters
on the moon of Yavin, and at the start of the next film have not only
relocated to the ice planet Hoth, but are ready to evacuate again.[38]
In *The Empire Strikes Back*, the Falcon evades the Imperials by
waiting until a Star Destroyer dumps its garbage, and floating out
with the refuse; an echo of their previous strategy in *Star Wars*,
when Leia blasts a hole in the wall of a pristine Death Star corridor
and the rescue team follows her into a trash compactor. The Rebels
not only discover the rubbish that the Imperials' sleek white surfaces
usually keep hidden; they immerse themselves in it and escape by
hiding in their enemies' waste, knowing the Empire will, primly,
never look at its own dirt.[39]

    A character's attitude towards trash, dirt and junk defines their
place on either side of the film's key opposition between rough,
improvisational energy and cold, clean formality, and the distinction
is not quite so simple as Rebel versus Empire. See Threepio 'can't
abide those Jawas. Disgusting creatures',[40] and Leia scorns the

bolted-together hulk of the Falcon: 'You came in that thing? You're braver than I thought.'[41] Some of this disdain can be put down to competitive banter between the kids and Han Solo – Luke calls the Falcon a 'piece of junk' because Solo has just humiliated him in the cantina, and Solo's blustering mockery of Leia ('The garbage chute, what a really wonderful idea! What an incredible smell you've discovered ...') is part of their ongoing, aggressive flirtation.

However, Leia and Threepio, despite their alliance with the Rebels, are not from the same sphere as Han and Luke, and this difference is expressed in their appearance and manner. Leia is a diplomat and adopted into the royalty of Alderaan, a peaceful and wealthy society; Threepio is a protocol droid on a consular ship, under the charge of an Alderaanian captain. Both characters, although Leia is secretly engaged in the overthrow of the Empire and Threepio has little understanding of his own position or the surrounding conflict, belong to the culture of the old Republic – a world of moneyed elegance, poise and etiquette – rather than the rougher world of Tatooine homesteads and Corellian pirates. Luke and his uncle, after all, are accustomed to buying their droids second-hand from Jawa junk merchants.

Luke and Han, making their way as a farmboy and smuggler respectively in Tatooine's dusty culture, have no political engagement with the Rebel Alliance until later in the story – initially, Luke just wants to get off-world through the Academy,[42] and tells Kenobi he can't get involved in any galactic struggle,[43] while Solo simply wants to clear his debts – but both have the instinctive hatred for the Empire born from the experience of a colonised, brutally policed people, rather than based on principle in an Alderaanian ivory tower. Luke exclaims 'it's not as if I like the Empire, I hate it', and Solo, who has just lost a hold full of spice and gained a price on his head because of an Imperial boarding party, lies automatically to the cantina stormtroopers, and shoots them dead without hesitation. Han and Luke begin the story as rebels by nature, rather than by conscious choice.

By contrast, Leia's mannered response to her capture by the Empire – 'I should have expected to find you holding Vader's leash. I recognised your foul stench when I was brought on board'[44] – is in keeping with the stilted conventions and delivery of Queen Amidala and the Jedi, in the prequel trilogy's Republican society, while Threepio's easily smudged gold plate makes him suited to Alderaanian palaces and clinical consular ships rather than farms and cantinas. Indeed, Threepio is redundant on Tatooine, and unnecessary, even offensive to its locals. Luke's Uncle Owen, a no-nonsense farmer, remarks disparagingly that he has no need for a protocol droid, while Obi-Wan, living quietly in a desert hut, can't remember ever owning a droid. The Mos Eisley barman even throws him out; he accepts hammerheads and walrus men, but not Threepio's kind. In Luke's first appearance, a scene deleted from the final cut, he owns a Tatooine-style robot – a primitive device called Treadwell, little more than a stick on wheels and light years away from the gleaming, humanoid Threepio. Threepio, cast out of his spacecraft into the desert, is not just on the wrong planet, but in the wrong film; he is a *Metropolis* (1927) robot in hopeless exile from the city, and wandering into *The Searchers* or *Lawrence of Arabia* (1962).[45]

Both Leia and Threepio, tellingly, are at home on the Death Star. Leia is undaunted by Tarkin and Vader, exchanging cold insults with her enemies, and even in prison, fits the clean white interior of the Imperial environment. Threepio just becomes another Death Star droid, and unlike Han and Luke, can talk plausibly to stormtroopers without any disguise or play-acting. On the other side of the conflict, the sandtroopers of Tatooine have adopted a customised uniform and trained native desert lizards, the Dewbacks, as police mounts; their white armour is scored and grubby with sand. They may not be a welcome presence in Mos Eisley, but they fit into the battered, improvisational milieu, just as Han Solo's antagonist Boba Fett, the bounty hunter with a uniform modified by trophies and scars, is his counterpart rather than his opposite.[46] The real opposition between the two key aesthetics of *Star Wars* – warm, rough creativity and cold, formal surface – is represented by Solo and Vader: they confront each other only once, at the precise middle point of the trilogy, in a Bespin dining room during *The Empire Strikes Back*. The moment presents another clash between different styles, between two of Lucas's borrowed genres – the dark-casqued samurai facing the cowboy – and offers a far more shocking contrast than the confrontation between Vader and Leia as political foes in the previous film, or, in the next film, between Vader and Luke as duelling Jedi.

Already, then, we can see that the fable of *Star Wars* allows for considerable ambiguity and movement between its polar oppositions, as signified through the relationship between two aesthetics: rough-edged versus smooth surface, raw energy versus order, and at its most basic, dirty versus clean. The narrative arc of the trilogy includes Threepio's loosening up until he can tell stories in *Return of the Jedi* and more significantly, Vader's trajectory towards his battered and burned redemption while Luke, more controlled, hard-edged and formal – with a mechanical hand under his black leather glove – comes dangerously close to replacing his father as the Emperor's soldier. Of course Leia and Han compromise into a couple, with him accepting the need for discipline and responsibility, and her becoming less rigid, more playful.

Even within the shorter story of *Star Wars* itself, Han accepts a role within the Rebel order, with everything that implies – the rituals of the Rebel Alliance are inherited from the old Republic, from Alderaanian custom, and as we shall see, are disconcertingly similar to those of the Empire – while Leia becomes more of a sassy wisecracker after joining Luke and Han's gang, most obviously when she improvises a route 'into the garbage chute, flyboy'.

Star Wars falls into three acts of unequal length. In the first, until the rescue team's entry to the Death Star, the Rebels and Imperials are physically distant, and we visit them in alternating scenes where the contrasting aesthetics are immediately obvious: the gleaming, black or white metal corridors of the Tantive IV or the Death Star, or the bustling, organic, adobe-and-sand environments of Tatooine.

The briefest glimpse of a freeze-frame would instantly reveal, from its colour scheme, whose world we are in, whether cold monochrome or warm earth.[47] As noted, Leia's formal dress and manner blends perfectly with the Imperial aesthetic at this point, and Threepio, though out of place in the desert, was deliberately designed to reflect the sand planet; the place where, in fact – though his memory of it is wiped – he was constructed in the prequel trilogy. As Lucas explains:

Leia is dressed in white and is part of the technological world – black, white and gray. She has a spaceship, but she would've been a stranger if she'd gone to Tatooine, the natural world: tan, brown and green ... [it] was a creative decision to make Threepio part of the people, earth side, which was an esoteric idea, but I liked it.[48]

The cold Imperial aesthetic; the warm earth tones of Tatooine

In the film's second act, the Rebels infiltrate the Death Star and subvert it from the inside on multiple levels: its architecture, its communications, its formal structure and uniform, but also in terms of the camerawork associated with the Empire. Lastly, the Rebels undermine the Death Star from the inside again, not by attacking it directly but by sneaking torpedoes into its exhaust port – as before, using the Empire's overlooked waste channels – and by adopting the military precision and discipline of their enemy. As noted above, it is this ordered ritual, inherited from the old days of the Republic through Alderaanian tradition, which unsettles any clear distinctions between the Empire and the Rebel Alliance in the final scene, and lays the seeds for the further complication of the boundaries between 'good' and 'evil' in the following films.

Tatooine's natural rock formations; the man-made world of the Death Star

This disruption of boundaries is the focus of my final chapter, 'Border Crossing'.

*   *   *

In May 1977, *Time* magazine described *Star Wars* as a compilation of '*Flash Gordon*, *The Wizard of Oz*, the Errol Flynn swashbucklers of the '30s and '40s and almost every western ever screened';[49] an analysis echoed in part and in a different context by Fredric Jameson's famous article from 1988 on the 'nostalgia mode', which explains the pleasure of the film in terms of its reinvention of the 'Saturday afternoon serial of the Buck Rogers type'.[50]

Indeed, my own previous writing on *Star Wars* has located the film's power and enduring influence in its distillation of icons, myths, motifs and occasionally, entire scenes from the greatest films of the twentieth century, from *The Wizard of Oz* (1939), *The Searchers* and *The Dam Busters* to *Metropolis* and *The Hidden Fortress* (1958); a rush of cinema in a super-compressed form.[51] This explanation also chimes with Umberto Eco's definition of cult film,[52] during his case study of *Casablanca* (1942) and its use of 'intertextual frames' and archetypes:

The term 'archetype' … serves only to indicate a preestablished and frequently reappearing narrative situation, cited or in some way recycled by innumerable other texts and provoking in the addressee a sort of intense emotion accompanied by the vague feeling of a déjà vu that everybody yearns to see again. […]

[With *Casablanca*] the authors mixed a little of everything, and everything they chose came from a repertoire that had stood the test of time. When only a few of those formulas are used, the result is simply kitsch. But when the repertoire of stock formulas is used wholesale, then the result is an architecture like Gaudí's Sagrada Familia: the same vertigo, the same stroke of genius. Every story involves one or more archetypes. To make a good story a single archetype is usually enough. But *Casablanca* is not satisfied with that. It uses them all.[53]

Star Wars uses them all, and in the figure of Han Solo, a one-man transit point at the corner of a bar in colonised territory, it also uses *Casablanca*.[54]

The powerful jolt of pure, classic cinema that *Star Wars* manufactured, concentrated and shot into the heart of a million seven-year-olds in 1977 goes some way, I think, towards explaining its immediate impact and effect. But it does not explain the longevity of the film's appeal – the immediate queues for repeat screenings, the laserdisc, video and DVD sales, the success of the Special Editions twenty years on, the official Expanded Universe of games, comics and novels, and the unofficial fan fiction, fan films and fan communities that continue to celebrate and explore *Star Wars* over thirty years since its first release.

The answer to this lies, I believe, in Eco's other requirement for a cult object:

The work must be loved, obviously, but this is not enough. It must provide a completely furnished world so that its fans can quote characters and episodes as if they were aspects of the fan's private sectarian world ... so that the adepts of the sect recognise through each other a shared expertise. [...]

A [cult] movie ... must be already ramshackle, rickety, unhinged in itself. [...] It must live on, and because of, its glorious ricketiness.[55]

Star Wars creates this sense of a 'furnished' world that we are only visiting; a world that was alive before we arrived, carries on in the background while we focus on the main characters, and continues after we leave. A handwritten note on Lucas's yellow pad, dating from early 1975, stresses this intention. '*Expand world* = behind every man must be a complete world. Customs, friends, enemies, goals, family, responsibilities, rules, religion.' His aim was familiarity tinged with strangeness:

a desire to re-create the feeling of disorientation he'd felt as a student watching films from different cultures. Lucas imagined what it would be like to watch a foreign film as if it had just washed up on the shore – all of its customs, history, language, and mannerisms strangely exotic, somewhat familiar, but not explained ...[56]

Specifically, Lucas had his own experience of watching Kurosawa in mind:[57] an immersion into customs that the characters understand, but that we, as visitors to the culture, must piece together. The status of a ronin and the reason he cannot take a follower, the importance of heritage and clan belonging, the code of honour in war; all go unspoken in *The Seven Samurai* (1954), and only become clear to the viewer in context, as the story progresses. The same is true of Godard's *Alphaville* – which directly shaped the design and culture of the Death Star – with its casually dropped references to Civil Control, previous and ongoing military conflicts and the mysterious Outer Countries.

Lucas had adopted the approach in *THX 1138*, whose rigid future world is also governed by enigmatic classifications and castes that the characters refer to in shorthand: 'I have to,' says LUH, 'he's a G-34', and we understand the general meaning if not the detail.[58] Even *American Graffiti* drops the viewer into a distinct culture with its own rules, cliques and quick-fire slang – 'If the prize is you, I'm a ready teddy.' 'Well, get bent, turkey.'

Star Wars, Marcus Hearn suggests, 'demonstrates Lucas' penchant for cultural disorientation',[59] and strives for 'a flawless evocation of an entirely imagined society'.[60] The key idea, according to Lucas, was that

you're introduced to a world you've never seen before. One of the premises is that I would assume this is a natural world for everybody, so I wouldn't dwell on setting this up, trying to explain what a droid is and so on.[61]

'George wanted spaceships that were operated like cars,' remembers producer Gary Kurtz. 'People turned them on, drove them some-where, and didn't talk about what an unusual thing they were doing';[62] while production designer John Barry explained that Lucas wanted the film to 'look like it's shot on your average, everyday Death Star or Mos Eisley spaceport'.[63]

Star Wars creates a world, then, where characters refer offhand to Bocce and to Tosche Station, to the T-16 skyhopper and the XP-38 landspeeder, without having to explain the background to us or to their companions. It is a world where Artoo-Detoo's carbon-scored bodywork, like Luke's battered speeder and the 'special modifications' Han has made to the Falcon, bear testament to previous adventures. It is a world where characters share knowledge of events long before the story took place, such as the Clone Wars, and of places we have never seen, and are never shown. Threepio mentions the Spice Mines of Kessel, and Solo, a spice smuggler, boasts about the Kessel Run, but the link is left to our imaginations.

And imagination has made those links, filled in those gaps. Kessel, never shown in the Star Wars saga, has been depicted in spin-off novels, fan films and PC games.[64] The Star Wars Encyclopaedia from 1998 retroactively explains Solo's apparent error in boasting that he'd made the Kessel Run in 'less than twelve parsecs',[65] while contemporary online sources like Wookieepedia go further, offering not just a detailed account of glitterstim spice's effects and derivation, but noting that one of the cantina band members, the Bith Figrin D'an, was an addict.[66] Thanks to official merchandise and amateur fandom we can now discover, in seconds, what the XP-38 looked like, what model it replaced and which Sullustan corporation manufactured it.

Arguably, thirty years of speculation and spin-offs, not to mention the three prequels with their graphic depiction of the Clone War, have filled in the gaps and 'fixed' the rickety text, reducing all its pleasurable mysteries to a dense but somehow uninspiring background. Perhaps fandom, and fan-driven Expanded Universe novels, have now over-saturated Star Wars with backstory and sequels – the extended saga currently includes not just the birth, but the death of Leia and Han's children – but in 1980, it was this sense of only glimpsing a rich, rough, diverse world that brought me into the ICA cinema with a notepad and felt pens, to frantically sketch and jot down observations from my second viewing. That, I believe, is what brought people back to *Star Wars*, and kept them involved in its mythos; the sense that there was much more to see and to discover. And this sense was almost entirely focused on the aesthetic I associated above with the Rebels, Han and Luke; the shabby, bustling world of Tatooine, where a vehicle's damage and a character's accessories – or a minor figure walking past the camera – suggest a wealth of other stories. A film centred on the Star Destroyer and Death Star – or indeed on Leia's consular ship – with their clean uniformity, identikit corridors and rigid patterns of behaviour, would offer far fewer hooks for further imagining, and gaps for speculation. Tatooine – which in effect is more the Rebels' base than the regimented, military HQ we later see on Yavin – is the focus of George Lucas's 'used universe' aesthetic.

According to Garry Jenkins, 'Lucas had a clear idea of the look he wanted' even by early 1975, when he asked Ralph McQuarrie to prepare the production art.

He had been struck by how dirty the Apollo missions had been when they returned from space. In his mind's eye he saw his corner of the cosmos as a grubby, lived-in place. Its technology may be more advanced, but it would not mean it could not break down, get rusty or need a visit to the interplanetary equivalent of a car wash. In his briefings to McQuarrie ... and his other design artists, Lucas had asked them to move away from the pristine world of the spaceships in 2001. His catchphrase was 'used space'.[67]

'George has this idea about a used universe,' recalled sound recordist and engineer Randy Thom. 'He wanted things in his films to look like they've been worn down, rusted, knocked about. He didn't want things to look brand new.'[68] Lucas explicitly told the design crew to 'dirty everything up'[69] – but only on one side of the conflict. 'George wanted all the Rebel ships to look secondhand, old and beat up,' said production artist Joe Johnston.'[70] He wanted them to look like they weren't as well built or well designed as the Imperial ships.' (The stormtroopers referred to below must surely be the Tatooine desert squad, rather than the spotless, polished Death Star soldiers.)

To emphasize the contrast between the gleaming black and gray of the Imperial fleet's interiors and the vessels of the Rebel Alliance ... they added rust and grease to the *Falcon* and other ships [...] technicians also nicked, scraped, scuffed, and scarred R2-D2, as well as the white armor of the stormtroopers. Before each take, actors rolled in the dust until their clothes looked as if they'd slept in them.[71]

This approach may have been initiated by Alec Guinness, who – as a veteran actor and a Knight of the Realm – was treated with reverence on the set, but who, perhaps remembering the sand-blasted, wind-blown aesthetic of *Lawrence of Arabia*, turned up for his first days' work, lay down on the desert floor and rolled around until his white robes were appropriately dirty.[72]

John Baxter suggests that Lucas's vision of a 'used universe' has its origins in the early 1960s, when Lucas started hanging around the car-racing culture of Northern California. In this 'new, pragmatic world ... all that counted were your skills, your capacity for action. Life wasn't for reflection: it was for use.'[73] Lucas, an academic under-achiever clashing with his father in a conservative small town, finally found something he was good at, and a potential escape from Modesto. He offered his skills as a mechanic and became the sidekick of a glamorous, older sports-car driver. The pleasures of taking things apart, understanding their workings and rebuilding them better made their way into *American Graffiti*, in the figure of hot rodder John Milner, and in turn, clearly shaped both Luke and Han Solo.

Luke, while dutifully obeying his uncle's restrictions and doing his chores, whether it's cleaning droids or staying on for another harvest, is clearly kicking against the boundaries of his flat, humdrum lifestyle: the only social scene is Tosche Station, a dull block of a

building in the middle of the desert where the listless local kids treat
Luke – or 'Wormie' – as an annoying pest.[74] With his big brother and
role-model figure – aptly, named Biggs – off-planet with the Academy,
Luke spends a lot of time alone, and clearly knows his way around
astromech droids like Artoo, as well as the Tatooine technology of
macrobinoculars, rifles, landspeeders and T-16 skyhoppers. A few
steps up the ladder, Han's successful career as a smuggler is based
around improvisation, creativity and an intimate knowledge of the
Millennium Falcon, from its hidden compartments to its unreliable
hyperdrive. Han's pride in his modified, customised heap of junk
echoes the teenaged Lucas's investment in his own first car: his dad
had caved in and bought a feeble Fiat Bianchina, which Lucas souped
up into 'an approximation of a lean, mean machine. The Fiat, never
very attractive, now looked ungainly and foreshortened – a "weird
little car", in the words of one friend – but George loved it.'[75]

On the production side, the *Star Wars* designers, model makers
and special-effects engineers also worked in a spirit of improvisation
and experiment, piecing together ideas from other people's junk
and testing the limits of newly constructed equipment, like a cross
between Chewbacca and the Jawas. John Dykstra even built a new
motion-control camera from bits and pieces of older machines. The
Dykstraflex could follow a precise trajectory towards, for instance, a
miniature TIE fighter, and then repeat the exact movement again to
capture the path of an approaching X-Wing. The two shots would
then be superimposed with other layers into a composite dogfight.
'We took archaic cameras,' Dykstra remembered, 'built before we
were even born, and we created hybrids of them by bolting different
parts together. Nobody else was inventing cameras to make films in
1975. We were there when a genre was being born and reborn.'[76]

The team at Lucas's new effects company, Industrial Light
and Magic, were engaged in a similar construction of hybrids,
'cannibalizing model kits in order to make spaceships. They used
fragments of Kenworth Tractors, Kandy-Vans, Panzer Kampf-
wagens, and even Ford Galaxy 500 XLs.'[77] A prototype of Vader's

outfit was 'a practical make-do amend', in the words of costume designer John Mollo: 'we put on a black motorcycle suit, a Nazi helmet, a gas mask, and a monk's cloak ... it was a little fashion show'.[78] John Barry describes how, searching for props, he went 'into the junk business'. 'The comlink is in fact part of a faucet. The handle of the lightsaber is a very old photographic flash unit ... Luke's binoculars are an old Ronoflex.'[79]

The sound design, masterminded by Ben Burtt, was also a creative composite and integral to the plausibility of the 'used universe'.

Lucas told Burtt to forget the electronic fizzes and sizzles of conventional science fiction soundtracks. As much as possible, all the sounds were to be natural. He wanted the spaceships' motors 'to sound real, to sound squeaky and rusty'.[80]

Burtt carried his Nagra tape recorder around the Los Angeles Zoo, LAX, military bases and his own apartment, composing a 'sound fabric' for *Star Wars*. He mixed the sound of take-offs, rifle ranges and strafing runs into an armoury of sounds for the Rebel and Imperial war machines, created Chewbacca's speech from a cinnamon bear, a walrus, seal and badger, and developed the threatening buzz of light sabres from, fittingly, the static of a TV set and the motor of a film projector. 'The sounds of the real world are complicated and kind of dirty,' Burtt explained. 'They simply cannot be reproduced on a synthesiser.'[81]

Lucas had stressed the importance of sound design to his films since USC, when he realised that an interesting soundtrack could draw students from the corridors into the screening room.[82] *THX 1138: 4EB* matched its visual superimposition of static, graphics and optical effects with a sound collage of garbled radio broadcasts and distorted signals,[83] and the feature version, even more ambitiously, privileged sound as equal to picture in a 'cubist' relationship. 'What we tried to do was detach the images; the stories and the themes, and the sound and the images, were all slightly different views of the same thing, seen simultaneously.'[84] *American Graffiti* also experimented with sound, using a different record as the backdrop to every scene and, as noted in the previous chapter, 'worldising' the sound through a makeshift process whereby Murch and Lucas walked in slow circles behind Lucas's house, one holding a microphone and one a speaker, recording the music in an open environment to introduce 'atmos' and realistic texture. This backyard experiment and spirit of home-made making-do is entirely in keeping with the creative collage of the Rebel aesthetic; the kind of attitude that buys a second-hand junk droid and fixes it up, or bolts special modifications and customised add-ons to a battered freighter.

To an extent, Lucas was also part of the inventive cannibalisation and poaching that created *Star Wars*; retaining a passion for editing, he had composed a prototype of the final dogfight sequences from every war movie he and Gary Kurtz could videotape from television,

so we had this massive library of parts ... *The Dam Busters, Tora! Tora! Tora!* ... *633 Squadron* and about forty-five other movies. We went through them all and picked out scenes to transfer to film to use as guidelines in the battle.[85]

In pre-production, of course, Lucas had patched together motifs, scenes, even lines of dialogue and character names from a range of sources, but during the often stressful and exhausting production process, he found himself in the role of distant manager, more a cold disciplinarian than a creative maverick – more an Emperor than a Rebel.

Lucas had been adamant that *Star Wars* needed his own special-effects shop with his own people, separate from Hollywood and its unions. 'That was one of the control things,' recalled ILM's Tom Pollock.[86] However, the crew, from Dykstra on down, were wild cards – Dykstra half-joked that his first requirement for ILM's Van Nuys offices was a swimming pool[87] – a motley crew of specialists like the Mos Eisley cantina regulars. Some were 'art or industrial design students', some were 'high school or college dropouts or burnouts', and only a couple were 'hired thanks to their unique skills', according to ILM production manager Bob Shepherd. 'In fact, almost all the people in the model shop ... were people I scrounged up wherever we could find them.'[88] Lucas's role as the innovative kid who broke rules and found new ways of making things work had been supplanted by the younger generation at ILM, who now enjoyed the luxury of creative goofing-off while Lucas wrangled with the responsibilities of direction. 'There was no dress code, no time clock and virtually no organisation. It was Dykstra's show – the crew's loyalty was largely to him, not Lucas.'[89] To Dykstra and his crowd, Lucas became the strict father, largely absent – until he turned up to check on their progress.

In summer 1976, Lucas visited the Van Nuys headquarters and found to his horror that 'ILM had already spent half its budget but had just one acceptable shot in the can'.[90] He was immediately struck by chest pains, was hospitalised overnight and emerged with a new determination to force production onward, even if it involved brutal streamlining. 'After more acrimonious discussions with Dykstra, and an appalled tour of the ramshackle Van Nuys installation, Lucas removed him from day-to-day supervision.'[91] Lucas's USC buddy, Matthew Robbins, commented that 'George, who was very much his father's son in terms of business, felt he was being ripped off.'

Lucas instigated a new, more rigorous regime, bringing in production supervisor George Mather to impose order, personally supervising ILM's work twice a week and sacking his editor, John Jympson. 'I tried to get the editor to cut it my way and he didn't really want to, and so I had to let the editor go. I was behind schedule,' the director remarked.[92]

Staff at ILM came to dread his arrival to look over the weekend's work. Progress was accepted without comment, failure with contempt. Passing people in the corridor, Lucas ignored them. To reduce conversations still further, he had three rubber stamps made up which he slammed on the drawings that crossed his desk.[93]

'Lucas was now the boss. His cool, calculating, sometimes remote manner could not have presented a starker contrast to Dykstra's free-wheeling philosophy.'[94] As a distant, cold and fearsome disciplinarian, tormented by his own chest pains as he strode the corridors, enforcing a strict timetable and sacking staff who let him down, Lucas had become the Darth Vader of *Return of the Jedi* who pays a surprise visit to the unfinished Death Star and growls at the commanding officer, 'I'm here to put you back on schedule.' The comparison is not just a neat conceit; it demonstrates Lucas's need for absolute control, and his discomfort with human interaction, which led him – despite his drive for rebellion against the old studio system, his creative, inventive streak, his penchant for getting his hands dirty with machinery, and his liking for the idea of warm, human community – to a fascination with and investment in the Empire, as well as the Rebels.

This central contradiction is most apparent in the documentary approach that shaped the filming of *Star Wars*. Lucas's fascination with documentary dates back at least to the summer of 1964, when he graduated junior college and hung around the race tracks filming with an 8mm movie camera – a gift from his father. To Baxter, Lucas's immediate affinity with observing life through a lens – and sometimes cutting out people altogether, to focus solely on objects – stems from his social awkwardness and anxieties.

Lucas discovered the pleasures of watching, ideally through the lens of a camera. People didn't ask awkward questions when you filmed them; they just let you be. And, seen through the camera, they themselves came into sharper focus. You could observe, comment, categorize, without saying a word. What Lucas found more interesting than human beings, however, were objects. [...] His early student films would all be about cars. He shot them from a distance and up close, noticing the reflections on a polished fender or

a windscreen; or clipped photographs from magazines and cut between them
to create a narrative that bypassed performance. The idea of directing actors
was, and would remain, distasteful.[95]

Lucas preferred to create his films alone, in isolation, through
editing, and he treated footage of human beings just as he had the
photographs from *Life* magazine that he had animated in his first
student short – as raw material to be given meaning in the cut.
During the 60s he was inspired by the new, raw and vibrant cinema
enabled by lightweight camera equipment in both the US and
France: the vérité documentaries of Robert Drew (*Primary*, 1960)
and D. A. Pennebaker (*Don't Look Back*, 1967) as well as the
freewheeling fictions of the French New Wave. Godard visited USC
for a guest lecture in 1966,[96] just when Lucas's interest in him peaked;
after that point, Lucas began to see Godard's cinema as unpolished,
and aimed for higher production values in his own work.[97]

While Lucas, in a characteristic contradiction, developed his
own style that combined rough energy with glossy surface and tight
cutting – his next film was *1:42.08* – USC's students and staff were,
Baxter reports, caught up in the new aesthetic. 'The fashion for hand-
held cameras, natural light, real locations and sound recorded "live"
spread through them like a virus.'[98] As Lucas's contemporary Randy
Epstein acerbically commented about the spirit of the time,

A real film-maker didn't write his or her film. They put a camera on their
shoulder, sprayed the environment with a lens; they Did Their Own Thing,
Let It All Hang Out, and anything they did was beautiful, because Hey, you're
beautiful.[99]

Lucas's talent for car mechanics, and his nascent interest in
film-making, had already led him into contact with cameraman and
racing *aficionado* Haskell Wexler, who, like the New Wave directors,
applied the hand-held, low-light and lightweight aesthetic of
documentary shooting to drama. Wexler's *Medium Cool* (1969), in

which a fictional story collided with real-life footage of Vietnam riots, prompted Lucas to consider a similar approach to a war film, shot when actual battles were taking place.[100] In the event, Coppola turned the idea into *Apocalypse Now* (1979), and Lucas went on to make what Walter Murch called 'a film from the future, rather than a film about the future,'[101] *THX 1138*.

The feature version of *THX* was, like the student short that preceded it, influenced by *Alphaville*'s use of contemporary locations to suggest a plausible future; partly for authenticity, and partly because it saved on the budget. Financial and time constraints, as well as aesthetic choices and his continuing admiration for vérité, shaped Lucas's guerrilla-documentary approach to his science-fiction narrative, but his decision to shoot scenes once, using multiple camera set-ups, was also prompted by his reluctance to deal with the actors and crew.

He shot as much film as he could of each sequence, using one camera for close-ups, a second for the master shot of the entire scene, and sometimes a third camera for another angle. Lucas rarely filmed a scene several times – occasionally he would film the rehearsals and print them. 'I'm very documentary in style, just set up the cameras and shoot the scene,' Lucas says. 'I like the actors to play against each other and not the camera, so I put the cameras off in the corner where they won't be intrusive.'[102]

Interacting with large groups of strangers was 'a concept foreign to Lucas', and his documentary distance enabled him to stand back on the margins. He tried to shoot his own first feature as he'd filmed *Mackenna's Gold*: from the sidelines. 'I'm not very good with people, never have been,' he admitted. 'It's a real weak link for me.' Actors were chosen who could work without close guidance, sparking off each other and developing their own performance. 'My life is too short to put up with a lot of trouble from my cast.'[103]

Lucas took the same approach to *American Graffiti*. Wexler lit the exteriors by boosting the available light – streetlamps and car headlights – and Lucas shot his cast of relative unknowns using a grainy stock, deliberately aiming for a grittily authentic feel.[104] The camera set-ups followed the pattern for *THX*, with two operators covering each scene, and the actors left to play their scenes as an ensemble with only minimal guidance from the director. 'I shot the film very much like a documentary,' Lucas explained.

I would set the scene up, talk to the actors about what was going to happen, where they were going to go and what they were going to do, set the cameras up with long lenses and let the actors run through the scenes with each other.

Actor Ron Howard recalled Lucas's distant style of direction and filming:

Often we couldn't tell where the cameras were. You didn't know if it was a long lens getting you in close-up at any given moment. If you asked George, he wouldn't tell you, and would just say keep doing the scene. [...] So at first it was disorienting – but ultimately it was incredibly liberating. When I saw the performances, I realized that he'd achieved a complete honesty and naturalism that made all the characters so real.[105]

In a seeming paradox, Lucas's physical and emotional distance led to a warm, authentic tone, with performers bouncing off each other, creating a group chemistry that the camera neutrally observed. Lucas then assembled the rough material into his story – the first cut was three and a half hours long – deliberately choosing the takes with accidents and minor flubs. The actors still remember Lucas instructing them to repeat a scene until they messed up a detail, then deliberately including that version in the final movie: the opening shot, for instance, shows Charlie Martin Smith failing to stop his bike in time and banging into a trash can, while Candy Clark fumbled her line 'did ya get it', and was incensed that Lucas refused to allow her another try at the dialogue. The last big ensemble scene after Bob

Falfa's car crash was shot while the sunrise lasted, in one take; the actors were left, unprepared, to improvise while two cameras rolled.[106] 'I wrote this script,' Lucas told them – not strictly true, as his stilted dialogue had been loosened up by Willard Huyck and Gloria Katz – 'so I'm giving you free rein to change any line you want. Say it how you'd say it.'

The rough-edged, natural warmth, chemistry and community of *Star Wars'* Rebel band was engineered in exactly the same way; by Lucas standing back and letting his cast, chosen for their sparky interactions during casting sessions, banter together. He announced in 1975 that during the casting for *Star Wars*, 'I'm looking for magic. What else can I say?'

Hamill and Ford 'condensed their lines to something like conversation' even in screen tests, and Ford in particular – notorious for telling Lucas 'you can type this shit, but you can't say it'[107] – improvised both his Han Solo costume[108] and several lines of dialogue. Hamill recalled that he was shocked when he first saw Ford's copy of the script, with lines crossed out and new dialogue in the margins. 'He had an amazing way of keeping the meaning but doing it in a really unique way for his character.' To Lucas, who knew he had little talent for writing natural speech – Huyck and Katz had reworked his final draft of *Star Wars*, too[109] – repeating the script word for word was not a priority.

Lucas's lengthy explanation of his intentions for *Star Wars*, again during 1975, demonstrates clearly that his approach was identical to the successful technique of *American Graffiti*, and that in many ways his ideas remained unchanged since the 1960s.

I'm trying to make a film that looks very real, with a nitty-gritty feel, which is hard to do in a film that is essentially a fantasy. [...] I like cinéma vérité; it's one of my real loves. [...] I like to have that edge of reality because I want the movies to make you believe they are real. I try to do it with the acting, too. It's more improvisational and linked to the style I use in directing, which is to have more than one camera and lead back away from the people, so that the actors essentially play the scenes themselves. The cameras are onlookers, and you aren't right in there. People aren't acting to cameras, people are acting to each other. I won't really demand that they get the lines right. They can play as much as they want with what they've got, which makes for a much more casual, sometimes much more intense interaction between actors rather than just having every little piece be perfect and done to the camera.[110]

As with *American Graffiti* and *THX*, Lucas relied on the stars to do their job, largely without his interference and guidance. 'If the part is cast properly and you have a really good actor, he can do it ... life is too short for crazy actors.'[111] In the central group of Hamill, Ford and Fisher, Lucas managed to recreate the playful energy of the French New Wave and the bantering camaraderie of a Howard Hawks Western or war film – not through the casual, laid-back camerawork of the former or the traditional approach of classical Hollywood, but simply by casting the right combination of actors and giving them a relatively free rein while his cameras observed them.[112] The deleted Tatooine scenes, edited by John Jympson in summer 1976 before he was sacked, give a sense of the lengthy, distant takes Lucas originally filmed:[113] a sequence showing Luke talking to Biggs about the Academy and the Rebellion covers the two actors in long shot and only cuts after one minute and twenty-six seconds. The introduction of Luke and his robot Treadwell opens with a nine-second extreme long shot of distant figures and a landspeeder, then cuts to a long shot, which it holds for a further ten seconds; in the original version of the cantina scene, the camera observes Han across the bar-room as a distant figure, obscured by the bodies of stormtroopers.

'In essence,' Jenkins suggests, Lucas 'had hired the leading trio to play themselves.' Hamill, in fact, modelled Luke on Lucas's softly spoken manner – he expected a rebuke, but the director simply judged it 'perfect'[114] – while the sardonic, arrogant Ford would announce on set that he intended improvising, warning Lucas 'Stop

STAR WARS | 45

me if I'm really bad.'[115] The scene where Solo ad libs his responses to questions on the Death Star intercom, then blasts the whole equipment deck – 'boring conversation anyway' – was invented on the spot, as was one of Ford's lines to Luke in the Falcon: ironically, 'don't get cocky'. While Fisher and Hamill took a more reverent attitude towards the script – Fisher, like her character, took the lines seriously at first, and rehearsed them diligently every night[116] – the hours of waiting around on the Death Star set with Ford bonded all three in a resigned fatigue that sometimes broke into manic hilarity, pranks and in-jokes; the making-of documentary *Empire of Dreams* (2004) shows Luke and Leia kicking their feet on the edge of a Death Star chasm, looking just like bored twins, and the gang in the Millennium Falcon cockpit whooping it up as though they're about to go on a family vacation. Their rapport overflowed into the scene where Luke first embraces Leia after the Death Star's explosion, and explodes in joyful squeals that almost sound like 'Carrie'; and into the final medal sequence, where their winks and grins threaten to disrupt the ceremony.

Lucas saw Skywalker as 'a pesky little brother' to Han Solo, and Leia as the annoying little sister – 'she's sort of a drag and she's a nuisance';[117] but in fact, rather than sibling banter, the off-screen relationships developed into sexual tension. Fisher and Ford, Baxter reports, 'became intimate … Hamill, hot for Fisher himself, was resentful'. Again, though Lucas had declared that he 'didn't want sexuality in his fairy tale',[118] his casting, rather than the direct influence of his direction, had inadvertently created the chemistry of a New Wave film: in this case, Truffaut's *Jules et Jim* (1962).

However, as with the ILM mavericks, Lucas remained remote, preoccupied and unamused by the actors' japes. Troubled by the film's slow and expensive progress, continuing wrangles with the crew and his own health problems, he failed to crack a smile when Ford pretended to munch on the scrap metal of the trash masher, or when Hamill sang out 'pardon me George, could this be Dia Noga poo poo?'[119] At the end of a take, he would call down from his position on a crane, with his characteristically curt advice: 'Faster and more intense.'[120] He was worried about losing control of the schedule, the effects and the sets – 'I cared about every single detail'[121] – and as bad luck plagued the making of *Star Wars*, Lucas became even more antisocial. On one particularly painful occasion, Hamill remembers, the director took his cast to lunch at a Chinese restaurant. 'Nobody said anything.'[122]

Again, then, this is one of the central paradoxes of *Star Wars*. Lucas had deliberately pushed himself, with *American Graffiti*, into making a warm, youthful, human movie shot using the naturalistic, documentary approach he had aspired to since his first student films. He was aiming for a loose, casual energy; the sense of community, energy and banter he had enjoyed and admired in the French New Wave, the American Western and war movies, and even in Kurosawa's samurai films. He achieved that tone by casting actors who could bounce off each other, creating group chemistry while the camera stood back and simply recorded. Yet Lucas was still deeply uncomfortable with social situations – even with a cast lunch, let alone sexual tension and risqué in-jokes – and the goofy banter of his cast, like the laid-back attitude of his ILM technicians, was just another threat to his control over production. Lucas was caught in a contradiction: he wanted that loose improvisational energy in the picture, but when it ran wild after the word 'cut', it disrupted his nervy need for tight organisation, and it made him anxious on a personal and professional level.

Lucas had successfully created, just by keeping to the sidelines and letting his actors do their work, what he called 'a kind of effervescent giddiness … a whole lot of humor and craziness'.[123] But he wanted to regain control, and solitude; and he found both in the editing room.

3 Order

George Lucas wrote *Star Wars* under a portrait of Sergei Eisenstein –
not Eisenstein on set, engaging with camera operators and actors,
but Eisenstein holding up a strip of film to the light; the director as
editor.[124]

   Lucas decided early on in his career that the editor was in
control of the film. His early influences at USC all, in diverse ways,
stressed the importance of cutting to the creation of meaning.
Vérité cinema, like Haskell Wexler's work and the French New
Wave, created stories from the raw material of street-shot footage,
developing Lucas's interest in documentary and documentary-style
fiction; the experimental animation of the Canadian Film Board,[125]
Stan Brakhage and Jordan Belson,[126] all of whose films Lucas
watched and studied in the mid-60s, relied primarily if not entirely on
the solitary labour of the artist-editor. Lucas's first student film, *Look
at Life*, demonstrated that movement, rhythm and a form of political
statement could be constructed by one young man, patiently cutting
and sticking short lengths of film together on a Steenbeck, with no
need for any other crew, actors, or human interaction.

   Look at Life was shaped most directly by Arthur Lipsett's visual
poem made out of documentary scraps, *21-87* (1964) – 'I was
extremely influenced by that particular movie,' Lucas recalled[127] –
but both Lipsett and Lucas's films could also be read as Eisensteinian
'intellectual montage'. The Soviet montage cinema was still revered at
USC when Lucas joined, not least because the previous Dean of
School, Slavko Vorkapich, had worked with Eisenstein in the 1920s,
and it directly shaped the curriculum. 'Vorkapich's influence was
everywhere at the school,' Lucas remembered. 'We focused a lot on
filmic expression, filmic grammar. I was not into storytelling. I was
into trying to create emotions through pure cinematic techniques.'[128]

Marcus Hearn recognises the combination of these different cinematic schools in *THX 1138: 4EB*. Describing it as a 'sophisticated successor to *Freiheit*', he identifies the film as 'clearly informed by the vérité and montage techniques he came to adopt while at USC'. Of course, in many ways these approaches to cinema were leagues apart, but Lucas found their overlap in the key role of the editor; a role which suited his two key motivations for absolute control, and for minimal interaction with other people. 'Let someone else work with the people,' was his attitude, according to fellow student Dave Johnson. 'People are just objects.'

It is the editor, Lucas learned, who determines ultimately what the filmgoer sees ... he sat for hours running long lengths of celluloid through his white-gloved hands, marking his cuts with a grease pencil, the scent of splicing glue dominating the small cubicle where he worked. To Lucas, writing or shooting a film didn't control the final product – editing did.
[...]
Lucas honed his editing skills because he was so weak at writing. He concentrated on visual films, abstract exercises, documentaries, and cinematic tone poems that could be constructed in the editing room, rather than on a typewriter. 'My feeling at that time was that scripts were for the birds,' Lucas recalls. 'I disdained story and character; I didn't have anything to do with them.'[129]

As discussed in my earlier chapter, though, Lucas did not restrict himself entirely to avant-garde experiment and documentary. *Freiheit* and *1:42.08* both rapidly draw the viewer into engagement with their central character, the boy sprinting for his freedom and the driver struggling against the racing car and his lap time. Both also draw on another form of editing; the template established by classical Hollywood, which focuses on a protagonist's emotional responses – aiming for an emotional, rather than an intellectual response in its audience – and creates a clear, coherent sense of the character's relationship to physical space.

   Similarly, *THX 1138: 4EB*, while it combines all the techniques
that Lucas had picked up during his undergraduate career – mixing
vérité and montage with the abstract imagery, static and shapes
of experimental animation – diligently follows continuity editing
conventions in the later sections, after a deliberately confusing
introductory sequence. We are, as in *Freiheit* and *1:42.08*, invited to
identify with the titular character through close-ups of his face, and
shots are linked according to Hollywood rules of spatial relations:
a controller peers into a scope, and we see his POV of THX 1138;
THX's race through an underground garage is constructed from mid-
shots and long shots linked through matching on action, keeping to a
consistency of direction; THX opening a door is cut smoothly with a
shot of THX entering a room. Perhaps significantly, the hero of *THX*
is also the editor – Dan Natchsheim played the main part, and then
cut the film.

   Note that while Lucas claims he was 'not into storytelling',
his stated aim was not, primarily, to evoke an intellectual response,
but 'to create emotions through pure cinematic techniques'.
Unlike Godard, Lucas had no intention of progressing to the more
Brechtian, self-reflective cinema of *Tout va bien* (1972); and Lucas's
first short animation is the closest he comes to the intellectual
montage of Eisenstein's *October* (1927). As *THX 1138: 4EB*,
Freiheit and *1:42.08* in particular demonstrate, USC had also
introduced Lucas to the work of D. W. Griffith, Alfred Hitchcock,
Orson Welles and David Lean,[130] and he cites William Wyler and
John Ford alongside Godard as two of his key influences in 1964.[131]
Even Kurosawa, whose work Lucas admired for its foreignness and
fascinatingly alien social structures, was a fan himself of John Ford;
The Seven Samurai is, on one level, an emotionally riveting action
film.

   Between graduation and the production of *Star Wars*,
three experiences hardened up Lucas's approach to editing, and
confirmed his need for absolute control over his work. In 1967,
Lucas was hired to cut a documentary about President Johnson's

trip to the Far East, and he resented the restrictions imposed upon him.

Editors had to discard footage of President Johnson's bald spot and the First Lady's prominent profile. Politcally, the footage had to be consistent with American foreign policy, and Lucas was criticized for the way he edited Johnson's visit to South Korea. [...] Lucas was angry enough to abandon a possible career as an editor: 'I realised that I didn't want other people telling me how to cut a film. I wanted to decide. I really wanted to be responsible for what was being said in a movie.'[132]

The experience showed Lucas that to retain control, he needed to shift his focus to direction. Yet he suffered greater pain when Warners took *THX 1138* from him, insisting on cutting four minutes. The edit was a deliberate power-play, a bullish response to Lucas's submission of an apparently uncommercial movie,[133] 'and in doing so, [Warners] turned Lucas' mistrust of corporate Hollywood into resentment'.[134] Like a recurring nightmare, history repeated itself with the completion of *American Graffiti*; even with Coppola furiously defending the picture during negotiations with Universal, the studio insisted on four and a half minutes of cuts.[135] To Lucas, it was worse than having a limb amputated; in a brutal metaphor, he compared it to watching his baby's fingers being cut off with an axe. 'They say, "Don't worry. Nobody will notice. She'll live, everything will be alright." But I mean, it hurts a great deal.'[136]

Lucas became even more determined to do things his own way, even if it involved making cuts of his own; and in this context it is easier to understand his decision to fire editor John Jympson.

I don't think he fully understood the movie and what I was trying to do. I shoot in a very peculiar way, in a documentary style, and it takes a lot of hard editing to make it work ... you want things to be right, and people will just not listen to you and there is no time to be nice to people, no time to be delicate.[137]

Lucas hired Richard Chew to start redoing Jympson's footage, and in the meantime, started cutting the Death Star dogfight scenes himself, with the help of his wife Marcia; because of course, George Lucas had even married an editor.[138]

'This was the moment Lucas had been working toward for more than three years – to have the raw material that he could meld into a cinematic experience.'

I really enjoy editing the most … it's the part I have most control over, it's the part I can deal with easiest. I can sit in my editing room and figure it out. I can solve problems that can't get solved any other way. It always comes down to that in the end. It's the part I rely on the most to save things, for better or worse. Everybody has their ace in the hole – mine's editing.[139]

Star Wars is overwhelmingly cut according to mainstream Hollywood convention. There is little confusion about the spatial relationship between characters or the consistency of their direction from one shot to the next. There are no jump-cuts, no direct addresses to camera and, with minor exceptions discussed below, no jarring violations of the 180-degree line. *Star Wars*, unlike some of Lucas's earlier work such as *Look at Life* and *anyone lived in a pretty (how) town*, and to a greater extent even than the more accessible narrative fictions of his student years, *THX 1138: 4EB* and *Freiheit*, follows the dominant conventions of continuity editing, designed to draw the viewer into the diegesis and keep him or her emotionally involved with no disruptions; the process of filming and editing is elided, made 'invisible'.

Indeed, *Star Wars* lifts shots, cuts and brief sequences from previous mainstream cinema, and they fit smoothly into the film, rather than shifting into a self-conscious stylistic homage. The scene where Luke discovers his aunt and uncle's homestead burning seems directly to borrow an alternating sequence of three shots (young man approaches and gazes in horror/long shot of the carnage from his point of view/back to young man's reaction) from Ford's *The*

Searchers, when Martin Pawley, who like Luke has been led away from the family home, returns to find it raided.

David Lean's *Lawrence of Arabia* seems to shape the framing and composition of several Tatooine sequences; the first shot of the desert expanse, with two small figures approaching down the frame over the dunes, is almost identical in both films, and Lean's depiction of the vast, empty terrain is echoed many times in the early scenes of *Star Wars*. Approaching strangers – a Jawa transport, or a Harith rider – are spotted miles away across the sand, as dots on the horizon; Luke – like Lawrence – uses binoculars to check the advance of distant Bedouin; and the view from a rocky outcrop over the bleak landscape – whether looking out towards Mos Eisley or Wadi Safra – is so similar in both films as to be virtually interchangeable.

Luke discovers the burning homestead; Luke's point of view

As a third example of direct homage, Michael Kaminski's *Secret History of Star Wars* website includes a detailed and fully illustrated account of Lucas's apparent borrowings from Kurosawa, including – as was the case with *The Searchers* – a chain of shots that seems lifted in its entirety from *The Hidden Fortress* and only minimally adapted. The duel between Darth Vader and Obi-Wan Kenobi, Kaminski demonstrates, follows the exact pattern of Toshiro's Mifune's staff fight:

The Searchers: Martin Pawley discovers the burning homestead; Martin's point of view

Lawrence of Arabia: desert landscape, distant figures; *Star Wars*: crossing the dunes;
Lawrence of Arabia: surveying the territory

Star Wars: looking towards Mos Eisley; *Lawrence of Arabia*: a rider approaching;
Star Wars: 'a transport, I'm saved!'

an establishing tableau, composed identically across both films, followed by a precisely matched rhythm of three subsequent shot/reverse shots as the opponents warily advance, and climaxing, in both cases, with the warriors' weapons clashing in diagonals across the frame.[140]

While Lucas has never confirmed whether the cases discussed above are intentional, shot-for-shot pastiches, he made no secret of the montage of war movies he used as a primitive 'animatic' to show the ILM technicians what he wanted from his space dogfights, and to serve as temporary footage while the effects were in production.[141] The official Lucasfilm documentary, *Empire of Dreams*, shows clips from unspecified war films alongside the sequence of the Falcon blasting through a TIE fighter pursuit squad on its escape from the Death Star, suggesting a direct, almost frame-to-frame correspondence between the shots. Abandoning Jympson's edit, Lucas asked Chew to prepare him a new rough cut, and then, in Chew's words, decided 'to get his hands dirty' and regain control over his film's meaning. 'It was too hard to explain what I wanted,' Lucas explained, 'so I just cut the whole thing.'[142]

The attack on the Death Star trench is clearly modelled on the final scenes of World War II movies such as *The Dam Busters* and *633 Squadron* (1964),[143] where a crack team of pilots faces the challenge of flying down a narrow passage under enemy fire from the ground and the air, to hit a small target with specially designed bombs and bring down a massive Nazi installation. The entire last act of *Star Wars* precisely echoes the narrative conventions of these two films in particular: the briefing, where officers display maps of the target and host a question-and-answer session, is followed by the milling camaraderie of pilots before take-off and then the attack run itself, which almost comes as a release. More specifically, *Star Wars* directly follows the editing pattern from these earlier films, building a suspenseful rhythm between POV shots from the cockpit, reaction shots of each individual pilot, exterior shots of the planes swooping (and crashing), and

constant reminders of the enemy cannon fire. The tension is heightened further by cross-cutting back to the control room, where officers and communication staff – and in *Star Wars*, Princess Leia – wait helplessly and follow the battle at a distance, through diagrams and radio messages; a technique that Lucas may have adapted from D. W. Griffith.

On an even closer and more detailed level, Lucas tried to recreate the movement of light in the cockpit shots of his war movies.

The one thing in the footage that makes it real is that the key lights change all the time. Even when they're just flying along in a straight line, the light is never sitting there. It's always rotating and moving. It's really a nice feeling, even if it's illogical.[144]

633 Squadron: mission briefing; *Star Wars*: Rebel war room

A close examination of the equivalent shots in *Star Wars* shows the effect in motion: within the space of a second, a key light slides up the shoulder of a pilot and over his helmet, dancing across the enclosed space of the cockpit.

In light of *Star Wars*' adherence to continuity editing and its direct, sometimes blatant borrowing from Hollywood or Hollywood-influenced cinema, it is easy to see why the existing histories of George Lucas's career represent it as a break from his earlier, 'experimental' work and a move into the mainstream. However, I have already suggested that the boundaries between Lucas's earlier work, his first two features and *Star Wars* are more ambiguous than might be supposed. Lucas had engaged adeptly with continuity editing since his student films, and all his features, from *THX* to *Star*

Star Wars: cockpit in shadow; changing key light

Wars, continue his early interest in documentary-style shooting: multiple coverage with distant cameras, leaving the construction of narrative and meaning to the editing room; an embracing of creative improvisation in his actors' performances; and of course, the sense of a 'used universe' that the movie visits briefly, only ever capturing part of its diverse and alien richness.

We can also see, in *Star Wars*, the continuation of Lucas's earliest experiments with sound layering – the echoing, 'worldised' tracks of *American Graffiti* and the 'cubist', contrapuntal audio effects of *THX 1138*, which in turn echoed the urgent soundtrack of distorted orders and reports in the original *THX* and the pontificating about freedom, filtered through radio static, that concludes *Freiheit*. In *Star Wars*, Lucas had Ben Burtt create a collage

633 Squadron: patterns of shade; light and movement

of familiar sounds in new combinations that, like the pieced-together props and the scuffed costumes, gives the sense of dropping in on a convincing, fully operational universe rather than a set at Elstree or an exterior crowded with crew members.[145] When Owen calls Luke for breakfast, for instance, we hear the gentle hum of moisture vaporators that form the constant, subliminal soundtrack to farm life on Tatooine. The Death Star has its own background rumble, the deep, thunderous workings of a machine the size of a moon, which is overlaid with anxious updates from its troops, some audible – 'We think they may be splitting up, they may be on levels five and six now, sir' – and some, like the surveillance reports in *THX*, merely a crackle of background conversation, a reminder of staff routines and system checks.

On a visual level, aspects of *Star Wars* also recall Lucas's student interest in formal experiment and abstract cinema. As noted, Lucas had encountered the new 'underground' cinema – Stan Brakhage, Jonas Mekas, Robert Breer and Jordan Belson – on his visits to San Francisco in the mid-60s,[146] at jazz clubs, in beatnik coffee shops and at makeshift screenings,[147] and had been introduced to the experimental films of the National Film Board – Norman McLaren, Arthur Lipsett, Claude Jutra – while at USC. Most obviously, Lipsett's *21-87* had inspired *Look at Life*, and McLaren's *Neighbours* (1952), a fable about the futility of war that uses stop-motion to animate its two actors, clearly inspired Lucas's *anyone lived in a pretty (how) town*, whose characters blip out of existence when photographed. The idea of actors as objects particularly appealed to Lucas, as will be discussed more fully below.

Star Wars contains at least one deliberate homage to this 1960s underground; Leia's cell block is 21-87. More fundamentally, Lipsett's assemblage of scraps into a montage poem seems to inspire Lucas's creative approach to collage, layering and found objects – whether pictures or sound, whether poached from existing sources or deliberately battered until they look like worn-out junk – and the work of the experimental animators showed Lucas that whole worlds could be created through a solitary, dedicated engagement with celluloid and an editing machine, with no need for actors or other interference. McLaren's *A Phantasy* (1952), for instance, depicts an unreal, ever-changing environment through cut-outs, while Brakhage plunged the viewer through inner and outer space by painting directly onto film and layering strips of celluloid together optically. Lucas would have seen his *Dog Star Man* sequence, which appeared out of numbered order – *Part I* (1962) was followed by the *Prelude*, *Part II* (1963), then *Part VI* and *Part III* in 1964.

This approach to cinema, with the editor as creator holding total control over the final result, in a direct and intense relationship with both picture and soundtrack, remained Lucas's ideal; the actual process of feature-film production was a painful compromise. What he really wanted was to transfer his ideas directly onto the film stock; and he wanted it enough to struggle through what, to him, was the horrific trial of working with actors, crew, effects teams and budgets. 'I always see images flash into my head, and I just have to make those scenes,' he said of his visions for *Star Wars*. 'By God, I want to see it. That image is in my head, and I won't rest until I see it on the screen.'[148]

CGI, finally, brought Lucas closer to this aim, allowing him to govern the construction of whole cities and crowds through computer simulation in the Special Editions and, to an even greater extent, the prequel trilogy. Yet even the original *Star Wars*, with its more limited technology, sometimes recalls experimental 1960s animation. All its sequences of ships hurtling through space, shooting bolts of energy at each other, are, after all, optically created through the layering of various film strips, just as Brakhage did with his cosmic, mythic collages or McLaren did with his *Mosaic* (1965), which superimposed two previous shorts. The laser shots and clashing sabre blades of *Star Wars* are simply rotoscoped – drawn on over the footage, frame by frame, as in Brakhage's or McLaren's animation – and the explosion of stars into radiating lines as the Falcon zooms into hyperspace recalls Jordan Belson's *Allures* (1961), which Lucas saw screened on the ceiling of the San Francisco planetarium.[149] The computer graphic displays that interrupt and comment on the Death Star trench attack – like the neon symbols and signs that crop up like a digital chorus through *Alphaville* – are also simple, animated diagrams of shifting geometry: circles overlapping with grids, dotted lines swooping through gaps.

For brief seconds, *Star Wars* shows us patterns of brightly coloured light, arrangements of shapes or psychedelic swirls. Paused during its sequences of galactic war, Jedi combat or hyperspace travel, it could almost pass for a work of abstract animation.[150]

These glimpses of Lucas's continued interest in experimental animation, in the middle of his first mainstream blockbuster, are

Entering hyperspace; blades of bright colour

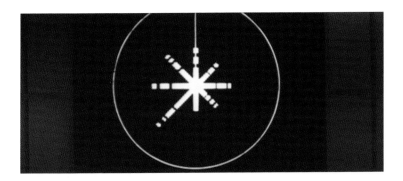

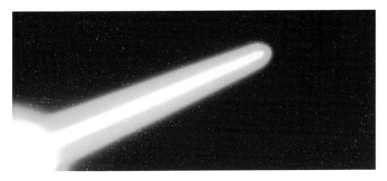

fascinating; but they are only brief glimpses, and even the sense of vérité documentary was reduced from the raw footage of *Star Wars* to the final cut. Richard Chew and George Lucas's editing tended to trim the long takes of the original shots – discussed in the previous chapter with reference to the deleted Tatooine sequences – to a far snappier rhythm. The Bazinian realism of the cut Tatooine scenes, where the camera simply watches neutrally from the margins for minutes on end, becomes a more Eisensteinian edit that, for instance, chops up the leisurely original takes of the cantina scene into brisk, lively montage. Kenobi's brief fight with the bully and his friend Walrus Man[151] is, in fact, cut according to the specific methods Eisenstein demonstrates in *Battleship Potemkin* (1925), where the combination of two shots (swinging sabre + injured opponent)

The Death Star in diagram; laser blast as abstract image

creates our understanding that the sabre caused the injury, without us ever seeing physical contact.[152] The idea that Soviet montage directly influenced Lucas's editing of *Star Wars* is not far-fetched: according to Rinzler, Lucas deliberately employed the Kuleshov effect[153] in the scene where Luke finds the burning corpses of his aunt and uncle. Hamill wanted to fall on his knees sobbing, but Lucas advised a quieter, more restrained performance, knowing that the joining of Hamill's blank stare with the POV shot of his destroyed home and family would, as Kuleshov had discovered, create the meaning 'shocked grief'.[154]

A sense of vérité's raw authenticity is still evident in some scenes, despite the efficient Lucas/Chew edit. The moments in *Star Wars* when Ford's playful departures from the script slip through into the final cut, and the winks and smiles between the central actors lend their scenes a warm, natural chemistry, retain a feeling of life observed and unaffected. There is also a rougher documentary feel to the unsteady shots when Luke or Artoo are being watched at a distance, through gaps in the rock, by Tatooine's bandits and scavengers, and also in the later Mos Eisley scenes; the first shot of Luke and his companions meeting an Imperial checkpoint is observed from across a busy street, with droids and passers-by, out of focus in the foreground, constantly blocking our view.[155]

For the most part, though, Lucas's approach to editing was tight, controlled and disciplined. Paul Hirsch recalls the test Lucas set him when he was hired to join Richard Chew: he was given a four-minute Jympson cut, and encouraged to use alternate takes not just to slice the scene down to three minutes, but to get 'more in it'.[156] As noted in the previous chapter, Lucas enjoyed the *idea* of loose naturalism. He liked the idea of the camera just hanging out on Tatooine, watching Biggs, Luke, Camie and Fixer chat and flirt like the young, beautiful kids in Godard while the camera watched them for as long as it took, and cut when the conversation was over. He liked it enough to shoot those scenes. They represented the part

Watching through the rocks; traffic passes the camera; Mos Eisley, documentary style

of him that had enjoyed the relaxed, laid-back gatherings of the 1970s, the part of him that tried to recreate the warm and mutually supportive film-making community of Coppola's American Zoetrope company.[157]

Yet Lucas found it difficult to maintain easygoing ideals while struggling with the emotional pressures and physical challenges of keeping his production on track; and just as he had become a remote disciplinarian on the set, barely dealing with crew or actors except to curtly approve or fail their efforts, so he approached the raw footage of *Star Wars* with harsh efficiency, paring it down until only glimpses of a looser, more casual cut remained. He was the 'general', as Richard Chew saw him, 'of this huge army'.[158] Again, though on one level Lucas genuinely identified with the creative, community feel of the Rebels – or the idea of the Rebels, although his social awkwardness had never allowed him to be fully comfortable with this kind of group in practice – the experience of directing brought him into far closer affinity with the cold, distant and alienated leaders of the Empire.

Lucas had already shown a talent for leading armies, far earlier in his career. For the USC version of *THX*, he assembled a team from the Navy and Marine Corps cameramen he had been teaching part-time. 'All at least ten years older than him, and mostly resentful of having anyone teach them their business, the sailors were contemptuous of almost all civilians, but particularly of hippie students.'[159] Lucas cannily marshalled them into two competing groups and set them technical challenges; the men responded with immediate and total loyalty. 'Within a week, those tough navy guys were licking George's boots,' said Dave Johnson. '... They were following him around like puppy dogs.'[160] John Milius judged it 'a brilliant piece of generalship'.[161] He was an efficient, no-nonsense leader, and becoming steadily more like his father, who had responded to Lucas's rebellious decision to go to USC by shrewdly offering him the tuition fees as a salary and keeping his son on the books as a paid employee.[162]

Military discipline, for Lucas, took much of the strain out of directing; a crew that didn't argue back or goof off eased the difficult process of getting the pictures out of his mind and onto a movie screen. In *THX*, he even reduced his actors – some of whom doubled as crew – to interchangeable, numbered drones, prefiguring the clones of the *Star Wars* prequel trilogy and the nameless, numerically coded troopers of the Death Star. If he had to work with people, he

THX 1138: 4EB: part of the machine; *American Graffiti*: gleaming bodywork

preferred to have them operating like cogs in a machine. Recall Baxter's comment that Lucas found objects more interesting than human beings,[163] and Lucas's own attitude, according to Dave Johnson: 'Let someone else work with the people ... . People are just objects.'

Lucas's first student films had celebrated the shiny surfaces of machinery – the leisurely reflections of *Herbie* and the yellow flash of *1:42.08*'s race car. In *THX 1138: 4EB* he put a bucket-sized helmet on an actor's head, hiding half his face, then labelled him '204' and sat him in front of a giant dashboard. In *American Graffiti*, despite his intention to make a warm and casual story about a group of kids, Lucas's camera lingered on the gleaming bodywork of parked vehicles.

Lucas found his objects of desire again in *Star Wars*, not in the beaten-up and patched-together accessories of the Rebels but in the polished, pristine aesthetic of the Empire: the clean, white armour that made the Imperial troops look like blankly identical robots; the perfectly drilled formations of those troopers, who in long shot became arrangements of white on black, patterns rather than people; the anonymous gunners who destroyed Alderaan, their identities shielded by casque-like visors that reflect only the lights of their control room, and of course Darth Vader, a man-machine whose

Surfaces of the Empire

moving parts, in this film, are entirely concealed in a gleaming black shell.[164]

George Lucas's first ever movie was a stop-motion cine film of plates, stacking themselves up and then unstacking.[165] He liked objects, and order, and control. He was, on one level, deeply invested in what the Empire looked like and represented, in its clean and shiny surfaces and its formal, rigid structure. But because he was trying to make a straightforward fable about good and evil, he had to let the Rebels' casual, careless improvisation into the structure he secretly admired, to disrupt it, and destroy it.

4 Border Crossing

Most [*Star Wars*] games, like the popular *Rebel Assault* CD-Rom, put the player in the position of a fighter in the forces led by the heroes … but the *Tie Fighter* game casts the player as a member of the Empire forces. As one adult player, a pony-tailed programmer from San Francisco told me, this recruitment into the forces of the Empire can be a source of intense fascination. 'I got totally identified with the Empire and its goals of maintaining order. I found myself hating the rebels because they brought disorder. It really freaked me out. I could see right away how I could become a great fascist.'[166]

This final chapter explores the conflict between the Rebel and Imperial approaches and aesthetics, which are kept separate, in alternating scenes between colour-coded worlds – cold monochrome surface versus rough, sandy clutter – until the Millennium Falcon enters the Death Star. The Imperials' capture of the Falcon ironically enables the Rebels' infiltration and subversion of the Imperial system; just as, in a later inversion, the Falcon's apparent escape from the Death Star finally leads the Imperials, via a homing beacon, to the Rebel base. In the film's final act, the Rebels employ military discipline to match and outwit the Imperials, and in the very last scene, the ritualised ceremony to crown the Rebel victory unsettles the distinction between the Imperials' association with 'order' and the Rebels' with casual, improvised creativity – setting up an uncertain relationship between these two apparent oppositions that will continue to trouble the sequel and the prequel movies.

George Lucas, like the 'pony-tailed programmer' who surprised himself by identifying with the Imperials, privately cherished the order of the Death Star, with its hierarchies, its structure, its neat shininess, its efficiency. It was the kind of system he wanted to be running; a system where telling people what to do was impersonal, like giving a machine instructions, where you could issue an order and know it's going to be carried out, with no answering back or goofing off. The Rebels, as the gamer discovered, disrupt that calm like a virus in a computer, like a disease within a body; like Lemmy Caution, the brash American agent, in the sterile European world of *Alphaville*; like Harrison Ford, Carrie Fisher and Mark Hamill on Lucas's set.

'We were all goofin' around,' Hamill admits on the making-of documentary, *Empire of Dreams*. 'And tryin' to make George crack, cause he really looked like he was ready to burst into tears.' We see the Rebels racing through a Death Star doorway, only for Lucas to mournfully tell them that the shot was ruined because of a microphone in frame. Ford and Hamill advance on the director chanting 'and? And? And?' then explode into disappointed groans, echoing 'the mike was in picture!' while Fisher whoops sarcastically. Lucas forces a pained smile. 'That, to him, was really inappropriate humour at the time,' Hamill concludes. ''Cause I'm sure he's in the zone, and seeing what he wants to do, and we're just like actors trying to stave off boredom.'

Yet Lucas, despite his own need for discipline and structure and his preference for objects over people, also wanted to make something that ran counter to those personal urges – something warm, human, fun and innocent – and so he let the Rebels run riot, while the Empire tries to control and at one point, literally crush them. The Death Star scenes are fundamentally about this conflict between two oppositional approaches, one of which comes naturally to Lucas, and the other which he struggles to embrace.

*   *   *

Though the Empire gains the upper hand by dragging the Millennium Falcon into its control with a tractor beam, Han and Luke's creative improvisation turns this imprisonment to their advantage. After inventively using Han's secret compartments to smuggle themselves, they successfully enter the Death Star system by disguising themselves

as soldiers with a Wookiee prisoner, becoming temporarily part of the
Imperial structure where people, for the most part, look like robots,
and non-humans are a despicable cultural other. 'Where are you
taking this ... thing?' spits the Imperial commander. 'Prisoner
transfer, from cell block 1138?' Luke replies helpfully. The Imperial
narrows his eyes. 'I wasn't notified. I'll have to clear it.' He signals to
his inferiors, helmeted troops who approach Chewbacca – and all
hell breaks loose.

The brief exchange demonstrates the Rebels' approach to the
rescue of Princess Leia and their subsequent escape from the Death
Star, which combines a subversive use of the system with a more
direct attack on specific nodes in the Imperial network. Luke, as we
see, adapts readily to the Imperial system of codes and numbers.
As the Falcon sits like a crusted rock in the middle of the clean-angled
Death Star hangar, we hear a constant background of announcements
in the Imperial discourse: 'Unlock 1, 5, 7 and 9. 316, report to
control.' Within seconds, Luke is dressed in trooper uniform and
taking the role of 'TK421', tapping his helmet to indicate a bad
motivator; he subsequently invents a cell-block number and sounds
plausible enough to convince a commander. Like Artoo, who can
plug into a single terminal and 'interpret the entire Imperial network',
obediently flashing up maps of the Death Star and its seven tractor-
beam locations, Luke speaks the Empire's language. He was, after all,
planning to leave home to join the Imperial Academy, before
presumably following Biggs's example and jumping ship for the
Rebellion; he knows about playing the game.[167]

Han, on the other hand, may have Imperial service in his
Expanded Universe history, but he turned his back on it long ago to
become an independent pirate and smuggler. His approach contrasts
with Luke's from the moment they infiltrate the Death Star. Luke opts
for disguise – he even keeps his mask on when rescuing the princess –
while Han and Chewbacca resort to brute force and blaster fire at the
first opportunity. 'You know, between his howling and your blasting
everything in sight, it's a wonder the whole station doesn't know

we're here,' Luke complains. 'Well, bring 'em on!' Solo replies. 'I prefer a straight fight to all this sneakin' around.' Right outside the cell block, Han hisses that Luke's plan is 'not gonna work'; while the Imperials run a tight hierarchy, the Rebel team – such as it is – bickers and gripes like kids on a family outing.

Of course, the plan does work, and Luke's strategy remains tightly pinpointed rather than randomly aggressive. Presumably following his previously agreed approach, he and Solo take out the Imperials in the cell-block control room, but then, as shown in a series of close-ups, they destroy eight separate cameras, damaging the clearly extensive surveillance system that – as the constant background commentary of checks and orders demonstrates – holds together Imperial discipline.

When Han is called on to deliver a status report himself, he is less adept than Luke at finding the right mode: he fumbles for official-sounding terminology, and when his improvisation about weapons malfunction and reactor leaks runs out, resorts to his blaster for an emphatic full stop, attacking the system rather than subverting it. He winces at his failure, realising he's brought more troops instead of holding them off as promised, but retains his clumsy, endearingly foolhardy approach; later he rashly blasts energy bolts off the magnetically sealed walls of the trash compactor, risking the ricochet, and chases troopers with a wild battle cry towards a dead end, buying time for Luke and Leia. 'He certainly has courage,' Leia muses. 'What good will it do us if he gets himself killed?' Luke replies.

Leia, like Kenobi – as already suggested – comes from a different world to Luke and Han. Kenobi has lived as a hermit since the days of the Old Republic, preserving the conventions of an era eighteen years earlier, when the Jedi flourished; Leia, as the adopted daughter of Alderaanian monarchy, has clearly grown up in a society that retains the Republic's cool formality and precise, elegant social rules. Though her family name suggests 'organic' and the military base she now calls home is a temple on a forest world, Princess Leia

Organa begins *Star Wars* as a self-possessed diplomat whose clipped diction and reserved manner – like her white gown and cinnamon-bun hairstyle – signify Alderaanian rules and ceremony, and give her more in common, initially, with the equally uptight Tarkin than with the lounging scoundrel Solo.

Kenobi, rather than changing, accepts that his time is over. His final scene is a formal duel with Vader, slow and careful like two men remembering the steps to an old, ritualised dance; it even takes place within a frame, in tableau as if on a theatrical stage. This is Obi-Wan's last performance.

Leia, by contrast, loosens up during the escape from the Death Star. As noted above, her trajectory throughout the trilogy crosses over with Han's as he becomes more socially responsible – both moving towards the point in *Return of the Jedi* where he accepts the position of military general and she dons a flowing, folksy dress in the Forest of Endor, and they can finally form the trilogy's romantic couple. It is Leia who orders Han 'into the garbage chute, flyboy', and though her attempt to pull rank as a princess and senator clashes with his stubborn self-sufficiency – he mocks her Alderaanian position as 'your worshipfulness' – by the time they reach the Falcon, she is bantering like a Howard Hawks heroine. 'Didn't we just leave this party?' Han grumbles, seeing his ship still

Kenobi's final battle

under guard; Luke and Leia arrive, out of breath, and Han barely glances at them as he asks 'What kept ya?' 'We, ah, ran into some old friends,' Leia shoots back sardonically. Like her earlier dig about the Falcon – 'You came in that thing? You're braver than I thought' – Leia's quick-fire dialogue and twangy delivery at the end of the Death Star episode are a world away from her earlier, tight-lipped ripostes to Tarkin and Vader.[168]

The Rebels' passage through the Death Star – Han and Chewie's violent assault in particular, rather than Kenobi's quiet journey[169] and Luke's more subtle infiltration of the system – obviously disrupts the Imperials' cold, clean and shiny *mise en scène*: blaster fire destroys the surfaces of consoles, revealing their smoking innards, and punches holes in the sleek, grey corridors, exposing the hidden garbage network. But it also plays havoc with film form. As an example, the early scene where Tarkin announces the end of the senate opens with a precisely symmetrical shot/reverse shot figure and moves through a smooth dolly that circles the round table. The camerawork here is both very much in keeping with the polished decor and the icy exchanges of the Imperials, and in direct contrast to the jerky shots with unfocused foregrounds when we cut to the Tatooine desert and the bustling streets of Mos Eisley.

However, the subsequent Rebel attack on the cell block breaks the room up into disorienting fragments – quick close-ups from diverse angles that make no effort to retain spatial coherence and, unusually, ignore the 180-degree line of continuity editing. It becomes almost impossible to keep track of who is shooting and in which direction; the effect is simply of choppy chaos. Similarly, the scene where Han defends the cell block after blasting the communicator begins with a shot of Chewbacca that – again in an unusual if not unique camera move within *Star Wars* – whip-pans across to Han as he shouts 'Get behind me, get behind me'. Solo's wildly destructive transit through the battle station, then, wrecks the staid and measured camerawork associated with the Imperials.

The Empire, in turn, or rather, its instrument the Death Star, attempts to exercise control over the Rebels not just by hunting and tracking them, but by literally crushing their resistance. The trash masher steadily reduces the space available to the Rebels, compressing the frame of the image into an ever-narrowing rectangle. The Rebels are, as discussed earlier, associated with junk and garbage, while the Empire is uniform surface: the image of the slick, dark walls closing down the cinema screen, squashing the improvisational, creative energy of the rescue squad – as they try every method available of blocking the walls – and compacting the messy, miscellaneous shapes of the *mise en scène*, with its dirty costumes, borrowed uniforms and constantly shifting layers of trash, is a perfect evocation of the opposition between the Imperial machine and the humans attempting to sabotage it.[170]

In the attack on the Death Star trench, we finally see the Rebels as a military organisation, rather than a small gang of adventurers. The Rebel system is less formal than the Imperials' – at the briefing, pilots politely interrupt their general, in an open dialogue unthinkable between a stormtrooper and his commander, and the Tannoy messages request 'all flight crews, man your stations' rather than directing people through alphanumeric code. Even the X-Wing call signs – Gold Leader, Red Five – are mixed with first names or

Crushing the Rebellion

nicknames such as Biggs, Wedge and Porkins, marking the Rebel army as more casual and human than its Imperial counterpart, where soldiers respond to 'TK421'.

The Rebels, then, move towards a middle ground in this sequence, between the previous, more clearly oppositional terms of rough, improvisatory creativity versus rigid, disciplined order. Luke is incorporated into the military system, taking on a uniform and a call sign, while Han, the rogue element, opts out and is excluded from this act until the finale. The attack on the Death Star is co-ordinated through diagrams and digital charts, echoing those we last saw within the Death Star itself; when the perspective cuts from the Rebels' graphic representations of the battle to those of the Imperials, only the more advanced, sophisticated Imperial technology distinguishes the two. The Rebel control room, where Leia nervously tracks the pilots' progress across these abstract diagrams of space, echoes with announcements that, again, are reminiscent of the Death Star interior. Rebel teams surrounded by winking lights and switches mirror their Imperial opposites in everything but the concealing, casque-like helmets: we are reminded of the Rebels as individuals, rather than as interchangeable, anonymous troops.

While the Rebel pilots retain a degree of informality – they are, after all, volunteering for this fight and flying alongside their buddies – their dialogue is terse and efficient, in contrast to the banter of previous scenes with the Death Star rescue gang. The X-Wing radios report 'Heavy fire, boss, twenty-three degrees,' and 'Three marks at two-ten'; Wedge exclaims 'Look at the size of that thing!' and is told 'Cut the chatter, Red Two.' Inside the Death Star, meanwhile, sirens wail and Imperial discipline is once again disrupted, with stormtroopers clattering and stumbling down the corridors; as the cannons fire, we even glimpse an Imperial gunner covering his ears and cowering. Hits on the battle station's surface explode into the interior, cluttering it with debris and blurring its clean lines with smoke.

Of course, though, the trench run is only successful because
Luke decides to fly solo, dropping out of the Rebel communication
network and its technological support system to trust in the Force,
and because Solo, by contrast, rejoins the group effort, rescuing Luke
at the last minute. Fittingly, our last shot of Vader shows the camera
spinning around his cockpit as he struggles for control, in a final
disturbance of Imperial order and a continuation of Han's disruptive
effect; and just as appropriately, Vader clearly regains his balance by
the end of that shot, sailing smoothly and defiantly, perfectly centre-
frame, into a clear black sky.

The blurring of boundaries between the previously clear-cut
oppositions of raw Rebel creativity and Imperial discipline is
emphasised by the very last sequence, the silent spectacle of the medal
ceremony.

Although Lucas claims that he had not seen *The Triumph of the
Will* (1935) for fifteen years before the making of *Star Wars*, and that
'the end of the movie is just what happens when you put a large
military group together and give out an award',[171] the composition
of the establishing shot is strikingly similar to Riefenstahl's
documentary celebration of the Nazi congress at Nuremberg.
Even leaving aside this specific parallel with historical fascism, the
sequence is surprising in its coding of Rebel victory as regimented,

The medal ceremony

ritualised, uniform, disciplined and ordered – precisely the qualities the film has previously associated with the Empire.

However, a spirit of play and improvisation creeps in as the main characters exchange glances in close-up; Luke struggles to keep a straight face but grins at Leia, who smiles back and tries to swallow it when Han smirks at her. As such, the Rebel gang introduce a sense of banter even into a silent scene, and threaten to sabotage the formality of the ceremony just as they undermined the Death Star's system. Lucas, of course, could have cut these shots where the cast's chemistry showed through, but he allowed, even embraced it, just as he welcomed a degree of improvisation and fumbled dialogue throughout his first three features, to provide the naturalism that, despite his best intentions, never came easily to him. In this scene, Lucas finally balances his preference for ordered composition and people as neatly arranged objects with his conflicting desire to capture natural warmth, humour and life unaffected.

Yet the medal ceremony has broader connotations in terms of the *Star Wars* saga, and Lucas's broader vision of the relationship between the two opposing sides. I have been using the word 'Rebel' for convenience, but this, within the story-world, is the disparaging Imperial term; the movement is more properly called the Alliance to Restore the Republic. Its purpose is to bring about a return to the era of the Jedi, represented in this film by Kenobi, and the elegant, formal society represented, at least initially, by Leia. By the last scene, Leia has lost some of her stiffness, and struggles to keep her composure; but this silent parade and medal ritual is clearly an attempt to recall and retain the customs of an older world, specifically the lost world of Alderaan.

Star Wars, through Leia and Kenobi, hints at what the Alliance is seeking to restore through its overthrow of the Empire. The Republic, we learn from Kenobi, allowed the Jedi to flourish as warriors and spiritual guardians; if we take Leia as representative of the society she is fighting to preserve and Alderaan as that society's last bastion, then the Republic was based around both monarchical birthright and a political senate – a senate which is dissolved at the start of the film by Tarkin – a culture of ritual (medals, ceremonial hairstyles) and precise manners, a world of diplomacy but also of hierarchical rank.

The prequel trilogy of 1999–2005 reveals this world in full detail, and also reveals Lucas's more complex design across the six films. The depiction of the Old Republic in *The Phantom Menace* is consistent with what *Star Wars* leads us to expect; it shows us the Jedi as a galactic police force, protecting a young monarch who subsequently becomes senator. Queen Amidala's dress, make-up, hair and manners represent a formal extreme, but the Jedi and the Republic's politicians are equally stilted and governed by strict codes of behaviour. The following two episodes, however, demonstrate that the ceremonial order of the Republic – with its elaborate, redundant social and political ritual – and the spiritual order of the Jedi, grown complacent and set in its ways, allows and enables the rise of the Imperial military order. Indeed, *Attack of the Clones* reveals that the Republic literally creates the Empire's army. The film's final sequence, a silent visual spectacle to a martial score,[172] recalls the *Star Wars* medal ceremony – and, again, *The Triumph of the Will* – as the camera sweeps over ranks of identical clone troopers. This is the Republic's army, and it fits precisely with their aesthetic of neat uniformity and grand ceremony, but it also, in an uncanny dynamic, both prefigures and echoes the rows of Imperial troops we remember from the original trilogy. Because the films were released out of their numbered sequence, the prequel scene gains a dramatic irony. We have already seen the episodes that follow, and know what the characters do not – that they are inadvertently building the Empire. The ships that rise above the ranked masses are not individualised, customised hot rods like the Falcon, but sleek daggers, prototypes of the Imperial Star Destroyers.

This perspective casts the end of *Star Wars* in a new light. The prequels show that the Empire grew from the Republic's order, and so the mission to restore that old system of structure and ritual, represented by the medal ceremony, seems like a return to the same

familiar cycle; and the ceremony itself, with its obvious parallels to the military rally that concludes *Attack of the Clones*, less of a cause for celebration. The New Republic will surely be little different from the Old Republic, which spawned the Empire – and in their shared penchant for hierarchy and rank within military, monarchic or spiritual orders, their displays of identical troops, their clean lines and symmetry, the systems offer little to choose between them.

This is the pattern suggested by Lucas's saga as a whole – not a straight clash between good and evil, or even the character arc of Anakin Skywalker's rise, corruption and salvation, but a cycle between apparently oppositional but in fact worryingly similar social structures, the Empire and Republic. Corruption, within Lucas's model, does not appear from outside, but festers within, emerging when a complacent society allows it to flourish; it can rise again if it is not checked and controlled, as Luke does with his urges towards hatred and revenge, or it can be exorcised, as Luke does by saving his father and destroying the Emperor. The original trilogy – and the six-film sequence – ends in *Return of the Jedi* with a looser, more playful celebration on another forest planet, but the question remains: is the Republic really worth restoring, and what, if anything, would prevent the process from starting again once Leia achieved her aim of rebuilding her parents' society?

Attack of the Clones: rise of the Empire

This concept of the Republic and Empire locked into a circular relationship over generations of galactic warfare – a struggle to restore the previous culture, which in turn created its own successor – suggests a bleaker picture than that of *Star Wars* itself, which as discussed presents a satisfying clash between clear-cut contrasts, and only unsettles those boundaries in its final scenes. The prequel trilogy is flat for this reason: it depicts one society, the Empire, emerging from a previous society, the Republic, whose members enable the rise of the new order precisely because the nascent Empire is too similar to the existing culture for it to be detected. Rather than the conflict on all levels that the cowboy Han Solo introduces when he enters the Death Star – in the actor's cocky improvisation, in his scruffy, customised costume and ship design, in the effect the character's presence has on the way Imperial interiors are shot and edited – we are shown well-meaning diplomats carefully debating policy with wily diplomats, highly trained Jedi in elaborately choreographed duels with highly trained Sith, computer-generated robots fighting computer-generated clones.

The prequel trilogy is a war of like versus like, order versus order. It represents the triumph of Lucas's drive for total control over his production, and the achievement of his aim to transfer the pictures in his head, with minimal interference, onto the screen. It represents Lucas's victory in containing and excluding the rogue energy of actors, special-effects mavericks and idiosyncratic crew members. It represents his triumph over the unpredictability of analogue camera equipment, mechanical props and real locations with their troublesome climates. It is hardly surprising that *The Clone Wars*, his feature-length spin-off of 2008, did away with those aspects completely and relied entirely on CGI.

Lucas's need for control, and his preference for an ordered system where he could work with objects – or obedient followers – won the battle. With the prequel trilogy, he achieved what one side of him had wanted since he first started making films. Perhaps he pushed aside or repressed the liking for naturalism, human warmth and documentary truth that also had shaped his earlier work, and in *Star Wars* had fuelled the central conflict; perhaps he convinced himself that those qualities were still present in the stilted humour and slapstick of the prequel trilogy's greenscreen actors and CGI monsters. Lucas's recent interviews, which obsessively rewrite the history of the production process and the saga's evolution, just as the series of Special Editions and DVD versions rework the detail of the narrative world, overriding and repressing any contradiction, are no longer a reliable document of his authorial intentions or reflections; but the 2005 documentary *Empire of Dreams* offers a moment of honest self-awareness.

What I was trying to do was stay independent ... but at the same time I was sort of fighting the corporate system, which I didn't like. And I'm not happy with the fact that corporations have taken over the film industry. But now I find myself being the head of a corporation. So there's a certain irony there, in that I've become the very thing that I was trying to, uh, avoid. Which is basically what part of *Star Wars* is about.

Lucas is, as he recognises himself, now closer to the Emperor than to the young director who made *The Emperor* in 1967. His vision of history in the *Star Wars* saga suggests that when one side achieves victory, it is only a matter of time before the cycle turns; and perhaps, as he has promised interviewers and colleagues but never managed, the other side of Lucas as a director will, now his grand saga is complete, come back into the ascendant.

It is now over thirty years since the first release of *Star Wars*. Lucas has got what he wanted; and arguably, lost much of what he had to offer. But in 1977, when he hated film-making but struggled through illness and arguments, overcoming his anxieties and pushing relentlessly to get those impossible pictures from his head to the screen, dealing with his own conflicting desires for human community and solitude, order and creativity, discipline and play, he somehow, not despite but because of the battle, achieved greatness.

Notes

1 Alan Arnold, *Once Upon a Galaxy: A Journal of the Making of The Empire Strikes Back* (London: Sphere Books, 1980).
2 Pam Cook and Mieke Bernink (eds), *The Cinema Book* (London: BFI, 2003).
3 David Bordwell and Kristin Thompson, *Film History* (New York: McGraw-Hill, 1994).
4 David Bordwell and Kristin Thompson, *Film Art* (New York: McGraw-Hill, 7th edition 2004).
5 John Hill and Pamela Church Gibson (eds), *Oxford Guide to Film Studies* (Oxford: Oxford University Press, 1998).
6 Joanne Hollows, Peter Hutchings and Mark Jancovich (eds), *The Film Studies Reader* (London: Arnold, 2000).
7 Thomas Schatz, 'The New Hollywood', in Jim Collins, Hilary Radner and Ava Preacher Collins (eds), *Film Theory Goes to the Movies* (London: Routledge, 1993), pp. 22–3. Peter Krämer, whose essay 'Post-Classical Hollywood' offers one of the few brief discussions of *Star Wars* in both Hill and Gibson and Hollows, Hutchings and Jancovich, promises more in *The New Hollywood: From Bonnie and Clyde to Star Wars* (London: Wallflower, 2005) but he treats Lucas's 1977 movie as the cutoff end point for his study, addressing it only in the final pages. Krämer's further essays, '"It's Aimed at Kids – the Kid in Everybody": George Lucas, *Star Wars* and Children's Entertainment', in Yvonne Tasker (ed.), *Action and Adventure Cinema* (London: Routledge, 2004), pp. 358–70, and 'Would You Take Your Child to See This Film? The Cultural and Social Work of the Family-Adventure Movie', in Steve Neale and Murray Smith (eds), *Contemporary Hollywood Cinema,*

(London: Routledge, 1998), pp. 294–311, demonstrate his sustained academic interest in *Star Wars*. His focus on the saga's articulation of family dramas and its consequent appeal to child and adult audiences is valuable, but his work seeks to discuss the films on a thematic level, rather than in close detail.
8 Geoff King, *New Hollywood Cinema: An Introduction* (London: I. B. Tauris, 2002), p. 135.
9 Robin Wood, *Hollywood from Vietnam to Reagan … and Beyond* (New York: Columbia University Press, 2003), p. 146.
10 Ibid., p. 147.
11 Ibid., p. 145
12 Jim Kitses, *Horizons West* (London: BFI, 1969).
13 Will Wright, *Sixguns & Society: A Structural Study of the Western* (Berkeley: University of California Press, 1975).
14 John Baxter, *George Lucas* (London: HarperCollins, 1999), p. 56.
15 Dale Pollock, *Skywalking* (New York: Da Capo Press, 1999), p. 70.
16 Baxter, op.cit., p. 70.
17 Sally Kline, *George Lucas Interviews* (Jackson: University Press of Mississippi, 1999), pp. 43–4.
18 Ibid., pp. 89, 96.
19 Ibid., pp. 110–11.
20 Kline, op. cit., pp. 110–11, 121.
21 Michael Kaminski, *The Secret History of Star Wars*, <www.secrethistoryof starwars.com/book.html>, p. 267.
22 Steve Silberman, 'Life after Darth', *Wired*, May 2005, n.p.
23 Ibid.
24 Baxter, op.cit., p. 62.
25 Garry Jenkins, *Empire Building* (London: Simon & Schuster, 1997), p. 20.
26 Ibid, p. 117.

27 Marcus Hearn, *The Cinema of George Lucas* (New York: Harry N. Abrams Inc., 2005), p. 33.
28 Pollock, op.cit., p. 101.
29 Cited in Jenkins, op.cit., p. 29; see also Kline, op.cit., p. 117, for a similar version of the same story.
30 Kline, op.cit., p. 38.
31 Ibid., p. 32.
32 Ibid., p. 116.
33 Ibid.
34 Kline, op.cit., p. 60.
35 Pollock, op.cit., p. 139.
36 Pollock, op.cit., p. 139.
37 Baxter, op.cit., p. 164.
38 In contrast to Grand Moff Tarkin, who dies, and presumably leads thousands of others to perish, because his pride will not allow him to evacuate the Death Star 'in our moment of triumph'.
39 Not for nothing does an Imperial commander refer to the Alliance, in *Return of the Jedi*, as 'you rebel scum'.
40 George Lucas, *Star Wars: A New Hope* (London: Faber & Faber, 1997), p. 52.
41 Ibid., p. 105.
42 Ibid., p. 18. Biggs Darklighter explains in a deleted scene that he is going to jump ship to join the Rebellion, rather than wait for the Empire to enlist him; the implication is that officially, the Academy is a training group for Imperial pilots.
43 Ibid., p. 46.
44 Ibid., p. 68.
45 Lucas explicitly called Threepio and Artoo 'the Metropolis robot and the Silent Running robot'. See J. W. Rinzler, *The Making of Star Wars* (London: Ebury Press, 2007), p. 37. Ralph McQuarrie's painting on the same page clearly reveals the resemblance, and masks in the style of Maria were actually made for actor Anthony Daniels; see p. 129.
46 It is Fett, tellingly, who follows the Millennium Falcon through the Star Destroyer's waste trail; like Han, he isn't squeamish about getting dirty.
47 See also Pollock, op.cit., p. 161, on this deliberate colour scheme.
48 Rinzler, op.cit., p. 247.
49 Cited in Jenkins, op.cit., p. 170.
50 Fredric Jameson, 'Postmodernism and Consumer Society', reprinted in Peter Brooker and Will Brooker, *Postmodern After-Images* (London: Arnold, 1997), p. 24.
51 Will Brooker, 'New Hope: The Postmodern Project of *Star Wars*', in Sean Redmond (ed.), *Liquid Metal* (London: Wallflower, 2004), pp. 298–307.
52 Matt Hills has characterised *Star Wars* as a 'cult blockbuster': see Hills, '*Star Wars* in Fandom, Film Theory and the Museum', in Julian Stringer (ed.), *Movie Blockbusters* (London: Routledge, 2003).
53 Umberto Eco, '*Casablanca*: Cult Movies and Intertextual Collage', in *Faith in Fakes: Travels in Hyperreality* (London: Vintage, 1998), pp. 200–2.
54 'Make Han in bar like Bogart – freelance tough guy for hire,' Lucas noted, around the start of 1975. See Rinzler, op.cit., p. 26.
55 Eco, op.cit., p. 198.
56 Rinzler, op.cit., p. 69.
57 Ibid; see also Hearn, op.cit., p. 113.
58 Lucas had originally wanted to shoot *THX* in Japan. 'It was a film from the future, rather than a film about the future,' says Walter Murch. 'We thought of the future as a country like Japan, and Japanese films were interesting to us, because they were made by a

culture for itself – and you learned about the culture by looking at that, but it didn't take any time to explain itself to you ... a Japanese film would just have the ritual and you'd have to figure it out for yourself.' See Hearn, op.cit., pp. 37–8.

59 Ibid., p. 112.

60 Ibid., p. 37. Lucas's term for this verisimilitude, 'immaculate reality', was also borrowed from Kurosawa; indeed, he had even considered using Kurosawa's mainstay actor, Toshiro Mifune, as Obi-Wan Kenobi, and casting a Japanese princess. See Hearn, ibid., p. 96, and Rinzler, op.cit., p. 68.

61 Ibid., p. 112.

62 Pollock, op.cit., p. 154.

63 Rinzler, op.cit., p. 65.

64 For instance, Kevin J. Anderson's *Jedi Search* (London: Bantam Spectra, 1994), Peter Mether's short film *The Dark Redemption* (1999) and LucasArts' PC game *Empire at War* (2006).

65 Stephen J. Sansweet, *Star Wars Encyclopaedia* (London: Virgin, 1998), p.162. The parsec is a unit of distance, not time. In the original screenplay, Ben 'reacts to Solo's stupid attempt to impress them with obvious misinformation'; see Lucas, op.cit., p. 57. The error is ironed out within current continuity by explaining that Solo negotiated a geographically short route, and so used the term parsecs appropriately.

66 See <starwars.wikia.com/wiki/Glitterstim>.

67 Jenkins, op.cit., p. 65.

68 Baxter, op.cit., p. 36.

69 Ibid., p. 196.

70 Rinzler, op.cit., p. 70.

71 Baxter, op.cit., p. 196.

72 Jenkins, op.cit., p. 106.

73 Baxter, op.cit., p. 36.

74 Even more depressingly, this minimal social scene exists only in the film's deleted scenes (and the novelisation).

75 Baxter, op.cit., p. 34.

76 Ibid., p. 177.

77 Kline, op.cit., p. 51.

78 Rinzler, op.cit., p. 112.

79 Ibid., p. 117.

80 Baxter, op.cit., p. 174.

81 Pollock, op.cit., p. 178.

82 Ibid., p. 46; see also Baxter, op.cit., p. 60.

83 Ibid., p. 68.

84 Hearn, op.cit., p. 38.

85 Kline, op.cit., p. 52.

86 Rinzler, op.cit., p. 80.

87 Ibid., p. 53.

88 Ibid., p. 90. See also Jenkins, op.cit., p. 133, and Pollock, op.cit., p. 171, for details of Dykstra's crew.

89 Ibid.

90 Hearn, op.cit., p. 130.

91 Baxter, op.cit., p. 214.

92 Hearn, op.cit., p. 105.

93 Baxter, op.cit., p. 216.

94 Jenkins, op.cit., p. 133.

95 Baxter, op.cit., p. 44.

96 Ibid., p. 54.

97 Ibid., p. 61.

98 Ibid., p. 52.

99 Ibid.

100 Ibid., p. 87. Lucas returned to this idea in 2002, with the digital simulation of hand-held footage in *Attack of the Clones*.

101 Hearn, op.cit., p. 37.

102 Pollock, op.cit., p. 91.

103 Ibid., pp. 91–2.

104 Hearn, p. 62.
105 Ibid., p. 64.
106 See Laurent Bouzereau (dir.) *The Making of American Graffiti* (1998); see also Pollock, op.cit., p. 111.
107 Baxter, op.cit., p. 189.
108 Ibid., p. 197.
109 Rinzler, op.cit., p. 132.
110 Ibid., p. 95.
111 Ibid., p. 188.
112 'Lucas usually filmed four or five takes of a scene … but they were long ones.' Pollock, op.cit., p. 163.
113 Hearn, op.cit., p. 106. Jympson's scenes were recut by Richard Chew, while Lucas and his wife Marcia worked on the Death Star trench sequence.
114 Jenkins, op.cit., p. 106.
115 Ibid., p. 124.
116 Rinzler, op.cit., p. 186.
117 Pollock, op.cit., p. 165.
118 Ibid.
119 Baxter, op.cit., p. 208.
120 Pollock, op.cit., p. 163.
121 Ibid., p. 168.
122 Ibid., p. 164.
123 Kline, op.cit., p. 119.
124 Baxter, op.cit., p. 153.
125 See Hearn, op.cit., p. 20.
126 See Baxter, op.cit., p. 44.
127 See Silberman, op.cit., n.p.
128 Hearn, op.cit., pp. 17–18.
129 Pollock, op.cit., pp. 53–5.
130 See Baxter, op.cit., p. 52; Professor Arthur Knight screened the work of Griffith, Welles and Lean. Hitchcock, Ford, Lean and other directors visited the campus to take part in Knight's celebrity interviews; see Hearn, op.cit., p. 20.
131 See Hearn, ibid.
132 Pollock, op.cit., p. 61.

133 See Baxter, op.cit., p. 108.
134 Hearn, op.cit., p. 43.
135 Ibid., p. 71.
136 Baxter, op.cit., p. 138.
137 Rinzler, op.cit., p. 196.
138 Hearn, op.cit., p. 106.
139 Rinzler, op.cit., p. 219.
140 Kaminski, op.cit. <www.secret historyofstarwars.com/kurosawa2.html>.
141 See Rinzler, op.cit., p. 230.
142 Ibid., p. 221.
143 Many war films were compiled into Lucas's guide montage: Rinzler, op.cit., p. 120 mentions *The Dam Busters*, *Tora! Tora! Tora!* (1970) and *Battle of Britain* (1969), while Jenkins, op.cit., p. 140 lists *The Blue Max* (1966), *633 Squadron* and again, *Tora! Tora! Tora!* See also Kline, op.cit., p. 52.
144 Rinzler, op.cit., p. 120.
145 Burtt uses the term 'worldising' to describe his approach to *Star Wars*, on the audio commentary to the 2006 DVD release: 00.14.30.
146 Baxter, op.cit., p. 44.
147 Silberman, op.cit., n.p.
148 Kline, op.cit., p. 44.
149 Silberman, op.cit., n.p. Belson's kaleidoscopic patterns in *Allures* also seem to inform the design of the exhaust shaft where Vader and Luke duel in *The Empire Strikes Back*, and the Republic senate chamber in the prequel films.
150 The climactic duel between Dooku and Anakin in *Attack of the Clones* focuses at length on the clashing, blue and scarlet blades rather than the combatants, and as such offers a more explicit nod to this 1960s abstraction.
151 In the Expanded Universe, they are named Ponda Baba and Doctor Evazan.

152 See Sergei M. Eisenstein, 'The Dramaturgy of Film Form', in Richard Taylor (ed.), *Eisenstein: Writings 1922–1934* (London: BFI, 1988).

153 Eisenstein and Lev Kuleshov had fundamental disagreements about the nature of editing, but nevertheless belong to the same broad national movement; Eisenstein saw Kuleshov's joining of shots into a sequence of 'blocks' as just one approach.

154 See Rinzler, op.cit., p. 149.

155 Lucas returned to the device of a hand-held, shaky camera, albeit digitally simulated, in *Attack of the Clones'* battle scenes.

156 Ibid., p. 226.

157 See Hearn, op.cit., p. 82, and Pollock, op.cit., p. 126, on Lucas 'Parkway' (Hearn) or 'Parkhouse' (Pollock) community and its symbolisation, to Lucas, of the 'Zoetrope dream'.

158 Rinzler, op.cit., p. 221.

159 Baxter, op.cit., p. 73. Ironically, Lucas's job was to 'loosen them up a bit'; see Hearn, op.cit, p. 22.

160 Baxter, op.cit., p. 74.

161 Ibid.

162 Ibid., p. 47.

163 Ibid., p. 44.

164 Vader's outfit actually became more reflective in the subsequent films, although of course his armour was damaged and his helmet finally removed. Lucas's formation of soldiers into regimented lines and patterns recurs more strikingly in *Return of the Jedi* with the Emperor's arrival, and most blatantly of all in the choreographed march of multiple, CGI troopers in *Attack of the Clones*, discussed more fully in the next chapter.

165 Baxter, op.cit., p. 24.

166 Janet H. Murray, *Hamlet on the Holodeck* (Cambridge: MIT Press, 1997), p. 147.

167 Significantly, Luke only makes it across the light bridge rope swing because he is still wearing the stormtrooper utility belt; Skywalker is more ready than Solo to adopt and use the enemy's tools.

168 Luke and Han also become more alike by the end of the film – Luke's costume at the medal ceremony is a version of Solo's casual belted and booted gear, while Han, in turn, pays at least token respect to Luke's new-found beliefs by telling him 'May the Force be with you.'

169 Kenobi's journey does, at one point, seem to disrupt the rigid formality of the Death Star. As he disables the tractor beam we overhear the banal conversation of two stormtroopers – 'You seen that new BT-16?' 'Yeah, some of the other guys were telling me about it. They say it's … it's quite a thing to see …' – an unusually naturalistic moment and a rare glimpse of the Imperial soldiers as regular Joes.

170 The sound design echoes this opposition, as the Rebels' screams, arguments and jokes battle against the relentless grind of the machine.

171 Rinzler, op.cit., pp. 296–7.

172 It is, in fact, the fullest rendition of the Imperial March we have yet heard in the prequel trilogy.

Credits

Star Wars

USA/1977

Directed by
George Lucas
Produced by
Gary Kurtz
Written by
George Lucas
Director of Photography
Gilbert Taylor B.S.C.
Production Designer
John Barry
Film Editors
Paul Hirsch
Marcia Lucas
Richard Chew
Music by
John Williams

©1977. Twentieth
Century-Fox Film
Corporation
Production Company
a Lucasfilm Limited
production
Production Supervisor
Robert Watts
Production Managers
Bruce Sharman
**2nd Unit Production
Managers**
David Lester
Peter Herald
Pepi Lenzi
Location Manager
Arnold Ross
Production Controller
Brian Gibbs
Location Auditor
Ralph M. Leo

Assistant Auditors
Steve Cullip
Penny McCarthy
Kim Falkinburg
Assistant to Producer
Bunny Alsup
Production Assistants
Pat Carr
Miki Herman
Continuity
Ann Skinner
Assistant Directors
Tony Waye
Gerry Gavigan
Terry Madden
Assistant to Director
Lucy Autrey Wilson
Casting
Irene Lamb
Diane Crittenden
Vic Ramos
2nd Unit Photography
Carroll Ballard
Rick Clemente
Robert Dalva
Tak Fujimoto
Camera Operations
Ronnie Taylor
Geoff Glover
Still Photographer
John Jay
Gaffer
Ron Tabera
**Special Photographic
Effects Supervisor**
John Dykstra
**Special Production &
Mechanical Effects
Supervisor**
John Stears

*Miniature and Optical
Effects Unit*
1st Cameraman
Richard Edlund
2nd Cameraman
Dennis Muren
**Assistant
Cameramen**
Douglas Smith
Kenneth Ralston
David Robman
2nd Unit Photography
Bruce Logan
**Composite Optical
Photography**
Robert Blalack (Praxis)
**Optical Photography
Coordinator**
Paul Roth
**Optical Printer
Operators**
David Berry
David McCue
Richard Pecorella
Eldon Rickman
James Van Trees Jr.
**Optical Camera
Assistants**
Caleb Aschkynazo
John C. Moulds
Bruce Nicholson
Gary Smith
Bert Terreri
Donna Tracy
Jim Wells
Vicky Witt
Production Supervisor
George E. Mather
Matte Artist
P. S. Ellenshaw

Planet and Satellite Artist
Ralph McQuarrie
Effects Illustration & Design
Joseph Johnston
Additional Spacecraft Design
Colin Cantwell
Chief Model Maker
Grant McCune
Model Builders
David Beasley
Jon Erland
Lorne Peterson
Steve Gawley
Paul Huston
David Jones
Animation and Rotoscope Design
Adam Beckett
Animators
Michael Ross
Peter Kuran
Jonathan Seay
Chris Casady
Lyn Gerry
Diana Wilson
Stop Motion Animation
Jon Berg
Phil Tippett
Miniature Explosions
Joe Viskocil
Greg Auer
Computer Animation & Graphic Displays
Dan O'Bannon
Larry Cuba
John Wash
Jay Teitzell
Image West

Film Control Coordinator
Mary M. Lind
Film Librarians
Cindy Isman
Connie McCrum
Pamela Malouf
Electronics Design
Alvah J. Miller
Special Components
James Shourt
Assistants
Masaaki Norihoro
Eleanor Porter
Camera & Mechanical Design
Don Trumbull
Richard Alexander
William Shourt
Special Mechanical Equipment
Jerry Greenwood
Douglas Barnett
Stuart Ziff
David Scott
Production Managers
Bob Shepherd
Lon Tinney
Production Staff
Patricia Rose Duignan
Mark Kline
Rhonda Peck
Ron Nathan
Assistant Editor (Opticals)
Bruce Michael Green
Additional Optical Effects
Van Der Veer Photo Effects
Ray Mercer & Company

Modern Film Effects
Master Film Effects
De Patie-Freleng Enterprises Inc.
Assistant Film Editors
Todd Boekelheide
Jay Miracle
Colin Kitchens
Bonnie Koehler
Art Directors
Norman Reynolds
Leslie Dilley
2nd Unit Art Direction
Leon Erickson
Al Locatelli
Set Decorator
Roger Christian
Assistant to Production Designer
Alan Roderick-Jones
Production Illustration
Ralph McQuarrie
Property Master
Frank Bruton
Costume Designer
John Mollo
Wardrobe Supervisor
Ron Beck
Make-up Supervisor
Stuart Freeborn
2nd Unit Make-up
Rick Baker
Douglas Beswick
Titles
Dan Perri
Music Performed by
the London Symphony Orchestra
(original music ©1977 Fox Fanfare Music, Inc.)

Orchestrations
Herbert W. Spencer
**Supervising Music
Editor**
Kenneth Wannberg
Music Scoring Mixer
Eric Tomlinson
Music Recorded at
Anvil Recording Studios
(Denham, England)
**Production Sound
Mixer**
Derek Ball
Re-recording Mixers
Don MacDougall
Bob Minkler
Ray West
Robert Litt
Mike Minkler
Lester Fresholtz
Richard Portman
Re-recording at
Samuel Goldwyn Studios
(Los Angeles, California)
**Supervising Sound
Editor**
Sam Shaw
Sound Editors
Robert R. Rutledge
Gordon Davidson
Gene Corso
**Assistant Sound
Editors**
Roxanne Jones
Karen Sharp
**Special Dialogue &
Sound Effects**
Ben Burtt
**Dolby Sound
Consultant**
Stephen Katz

**Post-Production
Completed at**
American Zoetrope (San
Francisco, California)
Stunt Coordinator
Peter Diamond
**Advertising/Publicity
Supervisor**
Charles Lippincott
Unit Publicist
Brian Doyle

Uncredited
Additional Dialogue
Gloria Katz
Willard Huyck
**Editor (during
production)**
John Jympson
2nd Unit Directors
Robert Watts
Gary Kurtz
Art Director
Harry Lange
Additional Alien Design
Ron Cobb
Sculptor
Brian Muir
Production Illustrators
Michael Minor
Alex Tavoularis
Construction Manager
Bill Welch
Make-up
Kay Freeborn
Graham Freeborn
Christopher Tucker
**Make-up Effects/
Design/Costumes**
Laine Liska
Michael Ignon

Hairdresser
Pat MacDermott

CAST
Mark Hamill
Luke Skywalker (Red Five)
Harrison Ford
Han Solo
Carrie Fisher
Princess Leia Organa
Peter Cushing
Grand Moff Tarkin
Alec Guinness
Ben (Obi-Wan) Kenobi
Anthony Daniels
See Threepio (C-3PO)
Kenny Baker
Artoo-Detoo (R2-D2)
Peter Mayhew
Chewbacca
David Prowse
Lord Darth Vader
Jack Purvis
Chief Jawa
Eddie Byrne
General Willard
Phil Brown
Uncle Owen Lars
Shelagh Fraser
Aunt Beru Lars
Alex McCrindle
General Dodonna
**Drewe Hemley [i.e.
Henley]**
Red Leader
Dennis Lawson
Red Two (Wedge)
Garrick Hagon
Red Three (Biggs)
Jack Klaff
Red Four (John 'D')

William Hootkins
Red Six (Porkins)
Angus McInnis
Gold Leader
Jeremy Sinden
Gold Two
Graham Ashley
Gold Five
Don Henderson
General Taggi
Richard Le Parmentier
General Motti
Leslie Schofield
commander #1

uncredited
James Earl Jones
voice of Darth Vader
George Roubicek
Commander Praji
Malcolm Tierney
Lt Shann Childsen
Pam Rose
Leesub Sirln
Shane Rimmer
InCom engineer

Dolby System
Technicolor
Prints by
DeLuxe
2.35:1 (Panavision)

The Producers wish to
thank the government of
Tunisia, the Institute of
Anthropology and
History of Guatemala,
and the National Park
Service, U.S. Department
of the Interior for their
cooperation.

Filmed from 22 March to
4 April 1976 on location
in Tunisia at a dry lake
bed near Nefta and at
the Hotel Sidi Driss in
Matmata; and from
7 April to 16 July 1976 at
EMI Elstree Studios
(Borehamwood,
England). Other exteriors
locations include the
Mesquite Sand Dunes at
Death Valley National
Monument (California,
USA) and Cardington Air
Establishment
(Bedfordshire, England).
Vista views filmed from
the upper landing of
Temple IV in Tikal
National Park
(Guatemala), 84 days
principal photography in
total.

US theatrical release by
Twentieth Century-Fox
Film Corporation on
25 May 1977 at 121m.
Rating: PG (MPAA:
24925). Re-released on
10 April 1981.
UK theatrical release by
20th Century Fox Film
Co. Ltd. on 27 December
1977 at 120m 50s/10,875
ft. Certificate: U (passed
30/06/1977 without cuts).

Some prints presented in
70mm (blow-up from

35mm) at 2.20:1 with
six-track audio.

Academy Awards for
Best Art Direction/Set
Decoration, Best
Costume Design, Best
Visual Effects, Best Film
Editing, Best Original
Score, Best Sound and
Special Achievement
Award (Benjamin Burtt
Jr).

Special Edition Credits

STAR WARS
Episode IV A New Hope

USA/1997

©1997. Lucasfilm Ltd.
Production Company
a Lucasfilm Ltd.
production

Executive Producer
George Lucas
Producer
Rick McCallum
Editor
T. M. Christopher
Sound Designer
Ben Burtt
Re-recording Mixer
Gary Summers
Assistant Editor
Samuel Hinckley
Sound Editor
Teresa Eckton
Assistant Sound Editor
Robert Marty

Re-recordist
Ronald G. Roumas
Digital Mix Technician
Gary A. Rizzo
Archivist
Tim Fox
Optical Supervisors
Phillip Feiner
Chris Bushman
Film Restoration Supervisor
Pete Comandini
Colour Timer
Robert J. Raring
Negative Continuity
Ray Sabo
Negative Cutter
Bob Hart
Post-Production Executive
Ted Gagliano
Special Edition Digital Remastering Provided by
Skywalker Sound (a Lucas Digital Ltd. company)
De-hiss Processing by
Cedar DH-1, HHB Communications Inc.
Film Restoration Consultant
Leon Briggs
Optical Restoration
Pacific Title
Film Restoration by
YCM Laboratories

Industrial Light and Magic
Visual Effects Producers
Tom Kennedy
Ned Gorman
Visual Effects Supervisors
Alex Seiden
John Knoll
Dave Carson
Stephen Williams
Dennis Muren
Joseph Letteri
Bruce Nicholson
2nd Unit Director and Cameraman
Joe Murray
Visual Effects Art Directors
Ty Ruben Ellingson
Mark Moore
Computer Graphics Supervisor
John Berton
Visual Effects Editor
David Tanaka
Digital Colour Timing Supervisor
Bruce Vecchitto
Sabre Group Supervisor
Daniel McNamara
Digital Scanning Supervisor
Joshua Pines
Visual Effects Coordinators
Margaret Lynch
Lisa Todd
Computer Graphics Artists
Karen Ansel
Mark Austin

Amelia Chenoweth
Terry Chostner
David Deuber
Natasha Devaud
Selwyn Eddy III
Howard Gersh
Paul Giacoppo
Joanne Hafner
James Hagedorn
Carol Hayden
Matt Hendershot
Guy Hudson
Stewart Lew
Jodie Maier
Greg Maloney
Stuart Maschwitz
Julie Neary
Kerry Nordquist
Scott Pasko
Damian Steel
Danny Taylor
Paul Theren
James Tooley
Chris Townsend
Timothy Waddy
Digital Matte Artists
Paul Huston
William Mather
Yusei Uesugi
Sabre Artists
Rita Zimmerman
Chad Taylor
Grant Guenin
Software Development
Christian Rouet
Rod Bogart
Brian Knep
Production Engineering
Fred Meyers
Gary Meyer
Marty Miramontez

Digital Plate Restoration Artists
Alan Bailey
Scott Bonnenfant
Corey Rosen
Negative Supervisor
Doug Jones
Assistant Visual Effects Editors
Angela Leaper
Forest Key
Scott Balcerek
Digital Production Assistants
Kela Hicks
Ronn Brown
Animatics Artist
David Dozoretz

CG Resource Managers
Nancy Jill Luckoff
Lam Van To
CG Production Manager
Suzie Vissotzky Tooley
Mixed & Recorded in a
THX Sound System Theatre
Special Edition Soundtrack Available on
RCA Victor
Novelisation Available from
Ballantine Books

[Added to] Cast
James Earl Jones
voice of Darth Vader

SDDS/Dolby/DTS Stereo Technicolor
Prints by
DeLuxe
2.35:1 (Panavision)

US theatrical release by Twentieth Century-Fox Film Corporation on 31 January 1997 at 125m. Rating: PG.
UK theatrical release by 20th Century Fox Film Co. Ltd. on 21 March 1997 at 124m 35s/11,212 ft +3 frames. Certificate: U (passed 13/02/1997 without cuts).

Credits compiled by Julian Grainger

Bibliography

Anderson, Kevin J., *Jedi Search* (London: Bantam Spectra, 1994).

Arnold, Alan, *Once Upon a Galaxy: A Journal of the Making of The Empire Strikes Back* (London: Sphere Books, 1980).

Baxter, John, *George Lucas* (London: HarperCollins, 1999).

Biskind, Peter, *Easy Riders, Raging Bulls* (London: Bloomsbury, 1998).

Bordwell, David and Kristin Thompson, *Film History: An Introduction* (New York: McGraw-Hill, 1994).

Bordwell, David and Kristin Thompson, *Film Art* (New York: McGraw-Hill, 7th edition 2004).

Brooker, Will, 'New Hope: The Postmodern Project of *Star Wars*', in Sean Redmond (ed.), *Liquid Metal* (London: Wallflower, 2004), pp. 298–307.

Bukatman, Scott, *Matters of Gravity* (London: Continuum, 2003).

Cook, Pam and Mieke Bernink (eds), *The Cinema Book* (London: BFI, 2003).

Eco, Umberto, '*Casablanca*: Cult Movies and Intertextual Collage', in *Faith in Fakes: Travels in Hyperreality* (London: Vintage, 1998).

Eisenstein, Sergei M., 'The Dramaturgy of Film Form', in Richard Taylor (ed.), *Eisenstein: Writings 1922–1934* (London: BFI, 1988).

Hearn, Marcus, *The Cinema of George Lucas* (New York: Harry N. Abrams Inc., 2005).

Henderson, Mary S., *Star Wars: The Magic of Myth* (New York: Bantam Books, 1997).

Hill, John and Pamela Church Gibson (eds), *Oxford Guide to Film Studies* (Oxford: Oxford University Press, 1998).

Hills, Matt, '*Star Wars* in Fandom, Film Theory and the Museum', in Julian Stringer (ed.), *Movie Blockbusters* (London: Routledge, 2003).

Hollows, Joanne, Peter Hutchings and Mark Jancovich (eds), *The Film Studies Reader* (London: Arnold, 2000).

Jameson, Fredric, 'Postmodernism and Consumer Society', reprinted in Peter Brooker and Will Brooker, *Postmodern After-Images* (London: Arnold, 1997), pp. 23–35.

Jenkins, Garry, *Empire Building* (London: Simon & Schuster, 1997).

Jenkins, Henry, *Fans, Bloggers and Gamers* (New York: New York University Press, 2006).

Kaminski, Michael, *The Secret History of Star Wars*, <www.secrethistoryof starwars.com/index.html>.

King, Geoff, *New Hollywood Cinema: An Introduction* (London: I. B. Tauris, 2002).

Kitses, Jim, *Horizons West* (London: BFI, 1969).

Kline, Sally (ed.), *George Lucas Interviews* (Jackson: University Press of Mississippi, 1999).

Krämer, Peter, 'Would You Take Your Child to See This Film? The Cultural and Social Work of the Family-Adventure Movie', in Steve Neale and Murray Smith (eds), *Contemporary Hollywood Cinema* (London: Routledge, 1998), pp. 294–311.

Krämer, Peter, '"It's Aimed at Kids – the Kid in Everybody": George Lucas,

Star Wars and Children's Entertainment', in Yvonne Tasker (ed.), *Action and Adventure Cinema* (London: Routledge, 2004), pp. 358–70.

Krämer, Peter, *The New Hollywood: From Bonnie and Clyde to Star Wars* (London: Wallflower, 2005).

Kuhn, Annette (ed.), *Alien Zone* (London: Verso, 1990).

Kuhn, Annette (ed.), *Alien Zone II* (London: Verso, 1999).

Lucas, George, *Star Wars: A New Hope* (London: Faber & Faber, 1997).

Murray, Janet H., *Hamlet on the Holodeck* (Cambridge: MIT Press, 1997).

Pollock, Dale, *Skywalking* (New York: Da Capo Press, 1999).

Redmond, Sean (ed.), *Liquid Metal: The Science Fiction Film Reader* (London: Wallflower, 2004).

Rinzler, J. W., *The Making of 'Star Wars': The Definitive Story behind the Original Film* (London: Ebury Press, 2007).

Rubin, Michael, *Droidmaker* (Gainesville, FL: Triad Publishing, 2005).

Sansweet, Stephen J., *Star Wars Encyclopaedia* (London: Virgin, 1998).

Schatz, Thomas, 'The New Hollywood', in Jim Collins, Hilary Radner and Ava Preacher Collins (eds), *Film Theory Goes to the Movies* (London: Routledge, 1993).

Silberman, Steve, 'Life after Darth', *Wired*, May 2005.

Taylor, Richard (ed.), *Eisenstein: Writings 1922–1934* (London: BFI, 1988).

Wood, Robin, *Hollywood from Vietnam to Reagan … and Beyond* (New York: Columbia University Press, 2003).

Wright, Will, *Sixguns & Society: A Structural Study of the Western* (Berkeley: University of California Press, 1975).